India
Through Virgin Eyes

India

Through Virgin Eyes

Keith Paulusse

www.whitefalconpublishing.com

India: Through Virgin Eyes
Keith Paulusse

www.whitefalconpublishing.com

First Edition, 2020

The contents of this book have been certified and timestamped on the POA Network blockchain as a permanent proof of existence. Scan the QR code or visit the URL given on the back cover to verify the blockchain certification for this book.

Requests for permission should be addressed to
Keith.Paulusse@gmail.com

ISBN - 978-93-89932-34-8

To my gracious Indian host the

Bhagat family of Beas

- Radha Soami -

Chapter Summaries

Readers are invited to access www.Indiathroughvirgineyes.com to view more pictures and information as well as interact with fellow readers and the author.

Chapter 1 Ajay, the soul of India

A serendipitous meeting

A psychology tutorial about intuitive awareness and mindfulness

A specimen of perfect manhood and spoken English

Transported into his intriguing Indian life

A self-funding student studying medicine

Survived on bread and butter, and walking 6 km to his carwash

Indian names fascinated me; they are nearly all celestial names

Their ability to ask penetrating questions; they viewed the world quite differently

Indians believe that our mind is our intellectual centre, the heart the emotional centre

How this extraordinarily Indian way was affecting their country

Chapter 2 The Quiet Carriage

Australian Indians are not Indian Indians

Australian Indian suburbs estimated a hundred thousand Indians live there

Dhruv and Shakti, the New Australian Indians

Is it apartheid or a deliberate Indian clannishness

Hindi mixed with "Hinglish", the type of English

Needs 80% pass marks to gain permanent residency status in Australia

Dhruv somehow has very low self-esteem, yet he, like Ajay, is a very good-looking, tall and handsome Indian from Punjab

No friends in the Indian community, they're always saying that he was not good enough

To find a wife, a Gay friend introduced him to many women

You're not in India now, Australian norms and values count here, not Indian

Chapter 3 The longing of our souls is always the longing of a lover

Travelling companions to thine own self be true

Mate, Matey, stereotypical Aussie

Introduction to the vibrant personalities of travelling companions

Secret ways to love and spirituality

Do not wink at Indian women and wear no shorts in certain villages

Going down being unauthentic

Chapter 4 It felt special and awesome being greeted by such a mix of novelty and curiosity that made this arrival in India so nice.

He was a population expert explaining the queuing process in India

Indians always have to compete for any space including personal space

Expensive male fragrance worn to make an impression, it attracts people like bees

The apartment looked like Art Deco with a slash of 'Indianese', we liked this Indian chic

Discovering that it was not uncommon for modern Indian families to often sleep together

The streets were spotless, being cleaned up by freely roaming mother pig and piglets

They were amazed that we westerners were vegan and did not take any animal products at all

Tey, our Priestly friend also lived around Cyber City and entertained in his smallish type marble temple

First impressions set the stage

Chapter 5 A personage of zenith beauty and perfection, an Avatar, I thought

The Punjabis from Northern India had an average of 26% and 15% DNA respectively from Aryan and Greek European people

Clutching Apples and Galaxies, as though they were newly evolved appendages to their youthful bodies

It is not becoming of a white face to sit with us on the curb

Embarrassed by my ignorance of Pehelwani wrestling, he invited me to a game of wrestling

I saw you gently stroking and talking to my sacred cow

Darius greets him with, "Hi, Polar Star" because that is the meaning of Krishna

That explained their physical and spiritual energy, perfect blemish-free skin, and the snow-whites of their eyes

You are now standing on the banks of the Beas River where the Greeks troops defied Alexander the Great in order to attack the Indians.

Chapter 6 With undivided emotion, Joyita showed the many pieces of popular Indian jewellery assisted by Das. Das was also gifted with the ability to see into the souls around

Jewellery acts as an agent of personality

Air-conditioned Arabica coffee – the smell of real coffee

Embarrassing Australian xenophobes
Jewellery has been an ever-present part of denoting culture and spirituality
Indian women wearing henna jewellery is vital to attract a lover
Earrings draw attention to erogenous ear lobes
Each Indian language and cultural group has its own design of jewellery like maagtika, nose rings
Aren't all humans peacocks? It is the soul that adds colour to our lives
Ayurveda medicine says women who wear a nath, experience less pain during childbirth
Indian men wear muscular bangles to enchant their sexuality and as a form of protection; it protects one from bad karma

Chapter 7 You are what you are, dear

Don't worry about them; they are Hijra, the third sex in India,
It is here where one sees deep into the human heart and soul
Hijra transgender people have a 4000-year-old tradition in Hindu culture
She kissed Darius on the forehead, with a holy kiss as to awaken the subconscious near the pineal gland
Australian transgender people and drag queens often look so much more feminine than the average Australian woman
The leader of the Hijra group did a past-life regression on Ajay who was a prince killed by the Greeks at the Beas river in 326 BCE, a son of the brave Raja Porus
Tikas and Mangalsutra were spectacles to behold a walking living cultural India all attached in one body.
In the temples of Jalandhar, there was something desirable and stunning for everyone
The Hijra are rising to their rightful place in Hindu society. Young Hijra such as Joyita Mondal at age 29 India's first transgender judge. First transgender police officer – sub-inspector Prithika Yasini

Chapter 8 India has lots of seasonings of affections to wit and here we were ending our journey on the oldest, longest, and one of the most magnificent man-made roads in the world

Looking after and caring for your elderly parents is a sacred duty and promised in the wedding vows

The narrowness of the streets was claustrophobic

Indian families do not get rid of their elderly in old age homes as they do so in the west

It is perfectly OK to sit in a room where people just sit in quietness and there is no need to talk

India shows a perspective of life like no other

Chapter 9 Beas Barbershop Conversations

Indian people ask us was what we thought of India and why do we appear to like them so much

We perceived that Indians are much more content and happier than most westerners

That's nothing, wait until you see the hundreds of thousands homeless people and beggars in Australia

4000 years old communal traditions and religion are the regulators of their collective minded society

At the Barber's shop, we would meet many Indian men with whom we could have talks serious and funny, and ascertain their state of minds.

India is a culture of science mixed with an equal portion of spirituality invented by great sages who were also great scientists

Beas was like a small microcosm of India; everything was made locally, everyone had a job either working for themselves or others.

Aunty Noona, the name of the dairywoman. She would fill her two-litre ladle to fill the canister full of unpasteurised milk, this would be 'tut-tut' in Australia

Chapter 10 Dera, a vision of future India

There was no need to set our clocks at four am; the Hindu Temples' choruses start chanting at 3 am

We were specially told not to wear shorts as we do in Australia, men's legs are apparently erotic

Taking a tuk-tuk, a type of motor rickshaw, three-wheeler was waiting to take us to the Dera town

Sitting so close that my nose almost rubbed her nose, she smiled showing rows of gold plated teeth

They are expecting three hundred and fifty thousand today as the Master Guru Gurinder Singh is giving a teaching

Thirty huge automated tea vessels, each producing 1120 litres of tea every hour

For lunch, one million flatbread Rotis, Chapati, Naan, Paneer, Dal and Dosa are made fresh

The whole Radha Soami organization is run by thousands of volunteers called Sewadars who offer Sewa (meaning selfless service)

The Dera library reminded me of the Alexandria library accidentally burnt down after the siege of Alexandria in 48BCE

They told us that in one week we were there, 46 kidneys, 30 human lungs and hearts plus 26 eyes were harvested

The design of these hospitals are 100% energy-efficient with natural light and fresh air, lawns and gardens

Chapter 11 a traditional Hindu wedding, big brash and beautiful

Hundreds attending, the gorgeous glamour of Indian imagery

Reception centre with a marriage feast fairground the size of an oval football field

Dancing inside it was explosively loud, Punjabi Rock Loud!

The aunties calculated the value of the wedding gifts for gossiping later

To take the seven steps of the saptapadi where they made vows to love and affirm each other and live happily ever after

The fourth Phera, the Bridegroom commit themselves by saying "Om mayo bhavyas jaradastaya ha" to respect and care for our elders and parents

Chapter 12 The Aunties, Mayla, Bedina and Mame walking matrimony sites

All seemingly like a mini version of the American comedienne Lucille Ball but the Indian versions

Whole village with real Aunts and Uncles raising nephews and nieces

Aunties would then transfer the wedding food into an ice cream container

Aunties were almost like drag queens in their character

Indulging in people-watching, making the appropriate or inappropriate comments of characters

And you, omg, hot hot, how many girls you westerners roam around with

Another aunty gives Ajay cooking advice, cleaning house advice and hygiene advice

A unique way of burning your ears and soul, life would not be the same in India without the aunties

Chapter 13 It's a destiny thing getting a wife or husband or partner for young Indians

Stomach bug Giardiasis parasite

Kartarpur sauntering amongst the Wallahs

Chatting at an El Fresco Fruit Juice Bar named "Juice Delight"

Getting a wife, "It's a destiny thing getting a wife for young Indians"

Social Media turned the Indian village into a megapolis

The newly acquired Indian global individualistic mindset

She feels like an Indian light beam when she does social media

Tinder is popular; Indian young people are members of virtual dating communities

Slowly diminishing Indian culture through the dumbing of homogeneity, the freedom of diversity and the end of the ever controlling consensus.

Chapter 14. Can you get me a Visa to Australia?

Indian young women – assertive, intelligent, wanting to make her own way in the world

Know Thyself, or to thine own self be true and it must follow, as the night the day

India is overpopulated especially in the cities and provincial towns, and there are few jobs for graduates

Indian young people should study in Europe, the Scandinavian Countries or The Netherlands

The British Commonwealth does not mean a thing, seven of their member countries are at the top of Human Rights abusers in the world

Australia dismantled her White Australia Policy and it took a good ten years to fully implement.

Backward, uneducated white people refuse to be seen by an Indian doctor and bluntly say they want a white doctor

Mental health issues are a big problem in Australia, don't get infected

Religion in Australia gets special privileges, Religious Schools – Christian, Hindu, Muslim schools receive more tax payer's money

We arrived in the middle of the night; were disinfected and provided with Australian food including foul-smelling sheep meat called mutton

Everybody attended information sessions on Australian law norms and values; it was best to conform to these entirely if you wanted to integrate successfully

In Australia, one does do not automatically get a pension

Yes, despite its entire shortcoming, modern educated Australians are way ahead of their backward and conservative politicians. It's one of the best countries in the world to live in.

Chapter 15 Comparisons are odious

Comparisons often come from a biased conscience filled with stereotypical ideas

In preparing ourselves for India, we watched many documentaries and films such as *Slumdog Millionaire*, that's the real India they said. *The Best Exotic Marigold Hotel*

They're keen supporters of Australia's Christian Prime Minister who, for six years, operated and continues to operate Australia's gulag of detention camps

They believe Australia should reduce its migrant intake especially Indian, Chinese and Muslims almost suggesting we should go back to the homogeneous *White Australia Policy, which* they view as the golden years of Australia

It was Sue and her Netball girlfriends who caused such a song and dance about our Indian postings "what about all the rapes in India"

"What about the beggars and homeless in India?" Sue asks. "What did you see in Melbourne this morning, Sue?"; "Well, yes, hundreds of people sleeping rough."

What about Child brides and child abuse, Sue said, not realizing that not too many years ago in Australia a twelve-year-old girl could marry. Sue was embarrassed about the recent *Royal Commission into Institutional Child Abuse*

Chapter 16 A magic realism hangs around The Sacred Golden Temple

A spiritual experience walking *Holy parikrama*

As an amateur historian, I drew parallels with history, religion and philosophies

The *Dukh Bhanjani Ber Tree* they said that the leaves have the power to cure any ailments

The *Adi Granth* was put to bed in an eighteenth-century English-like bed and covered with a blanket.

Ajay took us to the entry gate of Christ

This mysticism intrigued because it seems more like playfulness with our emotions

Not far from the Golden Temple was another massacre caused deliberately by the British on 20 April 1919 under the command of British General Dyer

Can you imagine the Roman Catholic Church in Rome providing meals to all tourists, it isn't happening; well, in India, at The Golden Temple, this is happening

Chapter 17 Train journeys and Diwali Festival

But the late-night train to Amritsar was third class and the fee was 300 rupees.

I felt like I was packed in a Nazi train on its way to a death camp, the heat and no personal space

These people were so poor they had not eaten since they left Mumbai 12 hours ago

Unlike Diwali, Christmas time in Australia is punctuated by the mass slaughter of animals and the enormous drenching of alcohol

Chapter 18 The head masseur introduced himself as Prosperity because everything he touched prospered

Where we are about to experience 4500 years of ancient health rituals

The all-white marble massage bathing rooms gave a peaceful and relaxed Zen feeling

Like metamorphosis, a whole new creation emerged of spirit, mind and body

Darius's skin and whole body felt sensuously scintillating, not unlike Amyl Nitrate effect on skin and veins, he had taken at the western health spas

The head masseur introduced himself as Prosperity because everything he touched prospered.

He took us into the *sacred knowledge room* where some incense sticks were burning and some males singing *shabads*

Hindu mythology has an infinite number of universes; in it, there is not one dilemma of modern man that has not existed before

Chapter 19 The Body Temple

Our purpose was to make love to the world as we encountered staggering secrets

Prosperity had introduced us to his friend Shiva, a young, vibrant Hindu scholar and PhD candidate researching ancient Vedic preventative medicine

We continued the exploration of ourselves with Shiva being the catalyst

We'd planned to ritually drink the ancient *Soma* nectar, a powerful priestly drink made from a mixture of secret herbs concocted by Shiva

An Indian Priest Physician called *Suruta* who first wrote about maintaining the Body Temple in 600 BCE and warned that corpulence and laziness is caused by lifestyle diseases

They strongly viewed the body as the focal point of human identity and that our spirits, consciousness, personalities and even God resides inside our *Body Temple*

The Hindus discepted disease and removed the supernatural such as demons from health and disease.

Thomas, a friend of mine with *Spina bifida* and Stephen Hawkins with *motor neurone disease*, both have brilliant minds and a great sense of humour, their Body Temple is as beautiful as anybody else's.

Indians, more than any other race that I had encountered, are thinkers and doers and most of them did not have a self-centred view of the world

From the Rig Veda, we learnt that *Indra,* also known as *Vishnu* or Zeus his Greek equivalent, was the supreme one God, the liberator of cows

Krishna introduces us to this 103 years old *Babaji* and wise Avatar, who has turned up from the Radha Soami community Satsang in Beas

Chapter 20 Conversations about Indian Identity and stereotypes

A Roman Catholic Italian woman and political leader, Sonia Gandhi made way for a Sikh, Manmohan Singh

Prosperity told us that India was actually an eclectic culture because it adopted many things from other cultures

The universe is the same for all of us, and different for each of us

In the west, our Indian Identity is of no consequence; it quickly dissolves

Religion is not practised as most of it is rationalised away in the far reaches of the conscious

The many-flavoured ice creams were scooped and served and licked by two blonde 17 and 18 years old women

To fit in, they use skin whitening cream in order to be more attractive to European women.

Take an *Apu* in The Simpsons, or the *Babu Bhatt* character in Seinfeld not to mention *the Kumars at No.42*. Do these families and personages represent India

Stereotypes don't just affect how people are perceived by others. Negative stereotypes distort how people view themselves

Chapter 21 An Ancient Indian Greek Symposium, Taxila – world's oldest 4000-year-old University

I felt like the Dionysus, the Greek God, coming out of India clad in multi-coloured silks, laden with bracelets and rings

New things we heard had been passed on via thousands of years of oral history

Encouraged to tap into the wisdom of the ages

Stunned that his name was Ganymede who was the lover of Greek God Zeus

The motto of the 4000-year-old Taxila University was *"Half knowledge is dangerous, seek for truth"*

It had a yearly enrolment of ten thousand students from all over the known world attended from as far away as Ancient Greece

The Darwinian Theory of Evolution fitted in perfectly with Hindu philosophy

In one day alone 66 million trees were planted by 1.6 million volunteers

There was already the beginnings of a participative democracy built upon people's trust

The facts are that most people on earth are trustworthy

The symposium showed that ancient Vedic literature records reveal there was already a participative democracy based upon trust.

Acknowledgements with Thanks

Australian-Indian meet-up group for use of their group picture in chapter 2.

My Facebook friend and fitness instructor, Singh Vicky, modelling Indian male Jewellery chapter 6.

To Mithu Das Das for his two cover photos.

To Theodore Bujor supplying the picture of Ro, Chapter 13.

The Age Newspaper showing homeless people sleeping in Melbourne, Chapter 15

Business Insider chapter 17.

News18.com, Sonia Gandhi picture, Chapter 20.

Character Descriptions

Ajay: He stood out in the way he carried himself, the body language emitting alluring vibes that could not be ignored.

Shakti: A celestial name meaning "energy of the Gods", a good looking millennial generation young Indian woman oozing with energy and enthusiasm about her new life in Australia.

Dhruv: A young 25-year-old Indian student graduating from Monash University with a Medical degree, who privately tells me he is in trouble. Dhruv somehow has very a low self-esteem yet he, like Ajay, is a very good looking, tall, handsome Indian from Punjab.

Darius, on the other hand, is a spiritual, sensual, fun-loving and a caring friend who loves health and fitness, especially the body-mind experience and anything to do with the mystery of consciousness.

Jag: Ajay's brother was like an American from Silicon Valley, confident and assured that nothing was impossible. The apartment built in the 1990s looked like Art Deco with a slash of 'Indianese', we liked this Indian chic, and we were up for a new experience of drinking genuine Chai Tea Latte.

Misha: Ajay's future sister-in-law when Jag interviewed her for a job. She got the job because it was love at first sight; their marriage was not arranged only through serendipity.

Darshan: Ajay's father who could no longer accept many of the social pressures that were contrary to his nature. He would never maliciously hurt any individual or cause any act that would suppress another's freedom.

Tey: A Hindu Temple priest in training. Enjoyed legal cannabis to be in touch with Krishna, one of the Avatars of the Lord Vishnu.

Krishna: Personage of zenith beauty and perfection plops himself next to me on the curb-side; simultaneously touching gently on my shoulder and greeting in a soft but strong attractive voice, "Hallo Keith, welcome to Amritsar."

Gurinder: An anthropologist told us that Indians are natural intruders into each other's lives, they see nothing wrong with developing intimacy with another person, even total strangers.

Chandragupta: A student of Indian history and named after the King who found the first Indian Empire, showed us where in 326BCE Alexander the Great stood, ate and slept.

Joyita: Our transgender jewellery designer took us into her atelier, a converted Hamman (Ancient Arab Bathhouse) into an artist colony for jewellers, fashion designers, sculptors, artistic painters, musicians.

Das Das: A personalized jewellery stylist, creating jewellery to bring out our best body features such as face, neck, ears, nose, legs, toes and fingers and the most desirable feature, your personality.

Nandini: The cook in our household, preparing many of the vegetarian dishes, was amazing; very different to my vegetarian cooking.

Aunty Bendina: Lovely and friendly, greeting Ajay for all to hear with a "my god, you have grown! Seemed only yesterday when you were wetting your pants."

Aunty Mame: She loved it when we spontaneously sang "you coax the blues right out of the horn, Mame. You charm the husk right of the corn, Mame.

Ro: The fruit Juice man, a recent IT Graduate. His whole appearance was carefully groomed, and like most Indian men, had perfect white teeth, tall and athletic, not inclined to slothfulness having the kind of demeanour that said, "at one with the universe."

Susah: A doppelganger of the famous Indian actress Anushka Sharma, all our senses are somewhat overwhelmed as we popped down in the seats taking in the fragrance.

Sonja: A 24-year-old woman, looking like an Indian version of the Italian actress *Gina Lollobrigida*, simultaneously joins our conversation saying she feels like an Indian light beam when she does social media.

Sangee: A pleasantly assertive, sparkling enthusiastic woman spontaneously asking us how she could fix a move to either Canada or Australia to live and study.

Vishal: An Indian medical doctor relating his experiences in Australia as a medical intern, experiencing discrimination at work especially in Hospitals, not from the staff but from backward, ignorant and slow white people.

Sue and her Netball girlfriends who caused such a song and dance about our India postings "what about all the rapes in India", our answer was what about all the rapes in Australia – we are fourth in the world for rapes and domestic violence and alcohol consumption.

Bill, Sue's husband, a businessman, asks "and what about the culture of corruption and bribery in India?"; "And what about it, Bill? Can you recall the recent *Australian Royal*

Commission into the Banks and its final conclusion that the Major Banks in Australia were corrupt to their core?"

Prosperity looked like a Greco Punjabi possessing desirable personality traits like enthusiasm, adaptability, patience humility, confidence, self-control, honesty and loyalty tied to some other interesting characteristics.

Rajeev: One of the masseurs; likes to deepen our insights about the law of attraction having ability to attract into our lives, whatever we are focusing on, in basic terms our thoughts turn things into reality, eventually.

Shiva: A young, vibrant Hindu scholar and PhD candidate researching ancient Vedic preventative medicine. He enamoured me by his splendidly designed golden leaf ear-cuff only worn by distinguished Hindu scholars, his many-sided protean nature, being adaptable and versatile in all things.

INTRODUCTION

India through Virgin Eyes

On returning from India, I felt like Dionysus, the Greek god, when he came out of India clad in multi-coloured silks, laden with bracelets and rings, his eyes ringed with black, his fingernails painted crimson. Dionysus, the god of ecstatic and a visionary, the god of wine and revelry of ascending life, of joy and action, of ecstatic motion and inspiration, of instinct and adventure and dauntless suffering, the god of song and music and dance. No, not everything in the world is evil and horrid; India was a healing salve, physically exhilarating and stimulating.

Life is all about people, and India has a lot of people, 1.3 Billion of them living in the world's largest Democracy that works. My visit to India smashed all stereotypes, none of them was true, and every perception that I had gained from mainstream news media and reading academic books were also far from true. You see, I went to India with Virgin Eyes that would perceive *perception as reality and truth.* Striving to look at the world as though one had never seen it before, a search for pure perception a fresh vision for me, I left my mind open and empty so to speak, realizing that if I freed myself of stereotypes and abstractions, I would live in a richer and more interesting world.

This book is not a common travelogue as you'll find in the travel supplements of the weekend papers. No, I don't go with that awful tourist idea that India is only a museum of antiquities and art. The Indian people are more marvellous than the land and temples.

The pleasure of entering other people's lives is an adventure into the glamour of Indian imagery, the ambrosia of their Gods and Avatars is everywhere. This story is told through the eyes of thirty real-life characters – funny, intelligent, clever, respectful; their every conversation being about destiny, with the past as guidance. I have changed their names for the sake of privacy and to protect the young ones against the annoying yet funny needling of aunties and uncles. My millennial generation travelling companions were my Indian friends Ajay, who had just finished his Education degree in Australia, and Darius from Telaviv in Israel having completed his Degree in Nutrition Science from Deakin University in Geelong, Australia. They're fun and smart young millennial types in their late twenties, fit and healthy vegetarians.

Firstly, this account is a positive, uplifting and exciting experience of India, written for the *Social Media Generation,* the ones who like short, punchy one-liners. You will not find any clichéd stereotypical Indian stories such as perpetuated by tourists and mainstream media like the traffic is anarchy, or their hyperbole about poverty, homelessness, the teeming beggars, the slums. No, I did not comment on these negatives because one sees plentiful of these in Australia as well. Nor did I comment on the corruption of banks and politicians, abuse of children by religion; we have plenty of those in Australia too. Secondly, I did not want to tread where many westerners have already trod, this is a journey of finding enlightenment in an ancient culture.

In India where the fantastic and the rich combine, it is here one sees deep into the human heart and soul because everything is right up close into your face. The chapters in this book contain much intrigue inspiring Indian otherworldliness, taking the reader's curiosities to an entirely new level. Much of it was written by being spiritually intimate with almost every Indian we mingled with. It is the people and their language that make a culture, so my aim was to meet and talk and listen to as many Indian people in their daily settings, meeting them serendipitously in the market place, in the Temple, in their homes and Ashrams, in the Dera's on farms and the market places, Body-Mind Retreats, Fitness Centres, Schools and Colleges, or drinking copious Chai (teas) and Bhaanlassie in Cafes on the curb-sides, while socializing, where else in the world but Amsterdam could you enjoy a super potent yet legal marijuana milkshake?

I followed my mentor *Stud Terkles,* a much respected oral historian who wrote many books such as *'A History of The Great Depression'* where he interviewed and lived with people across a wide spectrum of the social-economic status. Talking, sharing stories, asking questions, socialising at every level. Academics did not like his approach but the High Court of Canada determined that Oral Histories coming directly from the indigenous people passing their stories, myths and dreams, these stories were just as relevant as the Academic historical referential systems. All of the indigenous people have oral traditions; the whole of the Bible is an oral tradition finally written down in words. Often people's personal experiences count for more than anything else, they represent the truths for them.

Indian people whom I met were not as spiritually empty as so many are in the west; there was a collective indefinable pleasure in being so natural where men and woman expressed their fondness for each other in a completely natural way. Meeting the third sex, *the Hijra community* in India was special and very enlightening; these transgender people are part and parcel of the Hindu culture and religion.

'India Through Virgin Eyes' reads like a dramatic adventure novel but it isn't; it is much more powerful because it is real.

The style of writing is a stream of consciousness, narrating my way through the thoughts and feelings going on in the heads of the characters. These internal monologues with the characters provide a direct look into the "inner workings" of the thoughts and feelings of all the people we engaged with. This stream of consciousness provides direct access to the thoughts of characters, the inner workings of the human mind.

The Indians themselves did not always see what my virgin eyes saw, they had been seeing things for years and became jaded; they missed seeing the nuances, familiarity breeds content and contempt.

I am also trying to show a different India, than the one portrayed by the assimilating Indian Diaspora community here in Melbourne, and the Millennial Indian students who attended my school for over ten years and those Indians I encountered in chapter two on my train journeys. My Indian friends in Australia are annoyed at the stereotypes ascribed to them and sometimes racist taunts. I know what that was like as a Dutch migrant settling in Australia and first having to go to a Migrant Assimilation Camp to learn Australian norms and values and cooking. And it was frowned upon to speak a foreign language outside of the house. I asked if Indians in Australia today would put up with this.

Discovering the oldest university in the world was an exhilarating surprise. My Indian journey has come to an end, but not my Indian story, and not before attending an Ancient Indian *Plato-style symposium* where we met more extraordinary Indian people. Here at the symposium, I learnt that the present is what the past has produced, realizing that these Ancients Indians had superhuman intellects encrypted by a pearl of almost superhuman wisdom. Here, I learnt to pose questions that encouraged others to think beyond superficialities, think deeply what they care about and articulate their ideas.

'India *Through Virgin Eyes*' exposes and discovers aspects few people now talk about; there are many astounding stories, views and habits and historical statements given by Indian people telling their stories. I have checked these out using Google to see if history supports their views. I invite the reader to do the same and if curious about something, find out by Googling. However, in Googling, we create a conundrum I tend to check things up on Google, but what do I find? A fact, and a contrary fact or counter fact, then I look up an expert's opinion and what do I find? A counter expert opinion.

After meeting Ajay, my quest for more Indian cultural knowledge had begun, but it had to be knowledge attained through my personal encounters forming perceptions of reality in the moment, not necessarily gained from often contradictory academic writings, or sensational news report.

CHAPTER 1

AJAY, THE YOUNG SOUL OF INDIA

Meeting Ajay some nine years ago at a series of University tutorials about "intuitive awareness, mindfulness and centring" was a serendipitous encounter, spurning new consciousness and knowledge directly enhancing the quality of my life. He stood out in the way he carried himself, the body language emitting alluring vibes that could not be ignored.

It was not only Ajay but other Indian students who caught my attention that day. As a volunteer counsellor at a suicide prevention clinic, I was there to learn about mindfulness, as a few of my clients suffered from serious bouts of depression in the Victorian country where I lived. Hoping they too would benefit in practising mindfulness finding release from their constant ruminations blocking positive thoughts; I had come to the right place to learn.

My eyes and ears were immediately drawn to him talking and demonstrating breathing techniques. Here was a splendid specimen of manhood – tall, balanced muscularity, perfect Euro-Asian smooth skin, clear dark-blue eyes, strong white healthy teeth and a smile to charm the whole world with.

He appeared so aligned, sharing his vulnerabilities, augmenting his strengths, being comfortable in weaving all parts of his life together in a coherent way, here was an example of total self-actualization and a perfect balance of body, mind and spirit.

Suddenly, my mind switched into a déjà-vu mode as it often does in new surroundings, especially meeting new people. Had I met this man before? Maybe in another life, in my classical Greek life, was it just a quick flash of insignificant thought, did I say insignificant? His spoken English was perfect, only with a slightly sophisticated warm-sounding accent, unlike the heavily accented Indian Call Centre English. I could not immediately guess its intriguing origins. I thought he was a friendly noble Greek or Italian or maybe Spanish; he had that glow of a handsome race of people.

Ever since his lips broke into a friendly smile, we were destined to become friends. Immediately after our pleasant introduction, I was transported into his intriguing Indian life. Powerful introductions do this, don't they? One either makes an impression or not, it's the quality and genuineness of the impression. With an unusual amount of interestingly sustained eye contact, he looked straight into the windows of my soul confirming my feelings with his warm and firm handshake and an assuring pat on my shoulder. Telling me, he had recently arrived in Australia from Ukraine as a self-funding student where he had studied medicine, in the Russian language, no less. For various pragmatic reasons, he had chosen Australia primarily for its clean air and healthy fresh foods, more educational opportunities and diasporas of a large Indian-Australian community.

To financially support himself, he did modelling and acting work, having the skills and confidence in marketing, his obvious authentic personality, capitalizing successfully on his handsome looks and intriguing character. His other jobs were gym instructor and working as a "Bussie" boy in a famous South Yarra night club gathering empty glasses and collecting plenty of tips and salacious attention from the patrons.

The first three months in Australia were the worst because he had little money or friends, feeling isolated and vulnerable, surviving only on tea, bread and butter. Walking 6 km on his thongs because he could not afford the bus fare to his Carwash place of employment, working 10 hours per day, exploited at $8.00 per hour, his employer not paying tax or superannuation. He was soon asked to leave his shared house because he did not fit in with the pretentious lifestyles of his housemates. Temporarily, he felt alone and rejected, and yet despondency did not capture his spirit.

Without the full support of a mummy or daddy to fund his studies, he was reliant on his acute business ingenuity. It's no small deal to self-fund the thirty-five thousand dollars annual university tuition fee. Cleverly, he sublet his rented stylish three-bedroom South Yarra apartment as an Airbnb, attracting well-paying European customers, especially Dutch girls, he winked.

In all this he was practising ancient Indian mindfulness, strengthening his sense of resilience, being in tune with his sensations. Ajay clearly did not emphasize negative thoughts and overlooking the positive. All of this led to a sense of emotional, psychological and physical wellness in knowing himself and his place in the world, that and his sensuality drew people to his exuberance sense of ultimately him and others being in a state of bliss.

Indian personal names are not insignificant; they evoke empowerment, meaning, purpose, strength, energy, success and destiny: the name Ajay was a Royal Indian name denoting "invincible" together with his Royal bearing gave him this attractive vibrating air of confidence. These Indian names fascinated me; they're nearly all celestial names of avatars. Shakti, another Indian student said her name means "female energy" of God; *Amrik,* who was also in our tutorial, his name meant "celestial God", and *Jag*, Ajay's brother, his name meant "holy incarnation".

Indians are children of one of the world's oldest ancient continuing culture still practised today. This awareness and connection with the millennial past give Indians an edge in confidence, purpose and great faith in their future. Generally, multicultural Australians choose to remain ignorant in having any connection with their forty-thousand-year-old ancient culture, especially the Dream time stories of ancient Australian Aborigines that are akin to the ancient Vedic stories, the cement that holds India together. Sadly, this disconnect with the cultural past in Australia and in the West generally results in a national epidemic of depression, dysfunctionality out of all proportions resulting in no meaning or any connections with the universe creating a spiritual void.

Further out, what captivated me about Ajay and his friends was their intelligence, insights and empathy, especially their ability to ask penetrating questions. They viewed the world quite differently than most secular Australians whose major interests are sports and alcohol of any kind, particularly Football, Tennis, Cricket, they love Olympic torches and medals and are proud of Australia in being the number one gambling nation in the world. Indians are very different except they all seem to be cricket fanatics, surely a leftover from the British occupation.

It is evident to me that most of the Indian students were 'present in the moment', which, amongst other things, means that one becomes finely tuned to anything that does not feel quite right. If it feels crooked or not in harmony with nature, such as violently killing sentient animals, then they leave it out not letting violence captivate the mind. For these and a host of health and environmental reasons, they are vegetarians, being grounded in health-proven practices of thousands of years of Vedic spiritual, scientific and psychological teachings.

I had always been curious about the gut feel or intuition being more accurate than a supposed reality or situation. It intrigued me how the Indian students in this series of tutorial opened and warmed to "Intuitive awareness." Did they develop intuition or was it some latent psychic ability hidden deep in their Indian subconscious minds, or did they develop these psychic aspects themselves through education and cultural exposure? Ajay felt, after referring to the work of renowned psychologist Carl Jung, that fantasy and dreams are unconscious processes and are not hindered by intellectual defences and controls; in other words, one can increase both spiritual and psychic experiences by being open to them. "Young kids are naturally intuitive because they cannot verbalize as well as grownups. They stop using their intuitive perception especially in Australia's cultural values of reason and rationality, where mindfulness and intuition is often looked down upon. A great shame," the Indian students thought, intuition is valuable because it does not rely on what can be observed and can supply information one can't otherwise obtain.

Here, in my first meeting, I saw what humanity could be like Ajay and his fellow students showing ultimate health and beauty, stable minds, non-violence and having a collective mindset for the good of others as opposed to the West's fierce individualism concerned only with the 'me, me', and 'I, I', and little concern for the common good. I did compare all of this with the epidemic of depression and suicides especially in Australia and generally in the West. My quest for more Indian cultural knowledge had begun, but it had to be knowledge attained through my personal encounters forming perceptions of reality in the moment, not necessarily gained from often contradictory academic writings, or sensational news reports.

Ten years later, my life was never going to be quite the same again after that passport was stamped at Indira Gandhi International Airport, my journey in India had begun. I finally would experience and encompass the mysterious aspects of the inner world of the Indian consciousness all because of one serendipitous encounter, a spark that awakened my interest in Indian people and their ancient culture with all its mysteries attached.

These new Australian young Indians, full of enthusiasm and energy, could not keep quiet in the Quiet carriage when they boarded the train at the Indian Suburbs of Tarneith and Wyndham Vale. Shakti was one of these modern Indians whom I befriended.

CHAPTER 2

THE QUIET CARRIAGE

Not quite Indian, her clothes complimenting her body shape and her tulip-shaped exotic lips beamed confidence, intelligence and an innocence that exuded her sexuality; a work of art, I thought.

Shakti, a celestial name meaning "energy of the Gods", a good looking millennial generation young Indian woman oozing with energy and enthusiasm about her new life in Australia. We met in the "Quiet Railway Carriage" travelling from Geelong to Melbourne. This train stops at the "Indian" suburbs of Wyndham Vale and Tarneith; I say Indian suburbs because of an estimated hundred thousand Indians that live there. I am still figuring out whether there is a sort of voluntary apartheid or deliberate Indian clannishness of sticking together or if it's a fluke of developers building many housing estates.

I have made many new Indian friends who promptly sat next to me while travelling to my *School of Languages*; a broad friendly smile is probably taken as a welcoming invitation to sit next to me, not that they need my permission, a vacant train seat is anybody's with a valid ticket. Sitting in the Quiet

Carriage has many advantages, people are requested to switch off cell phones, listening to music using headphones is allowed as long as others cannot hear the sound. Quietness is essential for the sake of other passengers who want to emerge in the world of quiet and solitary, reading, gazing out the windows onto the pleasant countryside contemplating the *You-Yang Mountains* and seeing thousands of acres of golden wheat and yellow Canola fields, hundreds of sheep grazing in horizonless paddocks dotted by tall native Eucalypt trees providing shade for man and beast: ah, the bliss of sitting in the Quiet Carriage, with no intrusion of private, often annoying, phone conversations being broadcast at megaphone volume by some nasal trumpet sounding Australian Bogan.

Upon reaching Wyndham Vale, the quietness is usually disturbed by two groups of people entering the carriage, Australian Pensioners, who don't know what the word quiet means or they can't read the large print poster stipulating the rules for sitting in the Quiet Carriage, they talk continuously and loudly about their aches and pains and the high charges of electricity. The second groups are Indians and Chinese; they are like the pensioner groups and take absolutely no notice of the "Quiet Carriage" signs, when their usually loud phone rings, they must answer. I am sure many people do not understand what the word intrusion means; in this case, it means foisting your unwelcome noise on other people who wish to enjoy the quietness. I usually ask people who want to talk a lot if they are aware they're sitting in a Quiet Carriage, they listen with a 'surprise look' and then say, "Sorry, we'll be quiet, but we don't want to sit with all the noisy Bogans eating their smelly, greasy mutton meat pies and sauce *aromatizing* the carriage."

Shakti, a fashionable young Indian woman in her early thirties enters the carriage and as quick as a flash sits next to me. When her phone rings, she answers promptly in a nano-second speaking Hindi quickly mixed with "Hinglish", the type of English that has developed in India, in the same way as I often speak Dunglish, the way the Dutch speak English or Chinglish, the way that the Australian Chinese people speak English. I smile at Shakti gently pointing to the Quiet Carriage sign depicting the rules for sitting here. She smiles back and says, "I can read, but why don't you tell or point out to others who are talking, to be quiet too, instead of picking on me alone."

I get her message, simultaneously thinking, "Here is a sample of the new breed of young, assertive Australian Indian women. You can never tell Indians to be quiet." Shakti asserts, "They just won't, they love chatting," she did have a point resigning myself to the fact that I cannot police the Quiet Carriage by myself, it's full of millennials switched on to a sound so loud, you could run a disco. Relaxing a little, no doubt to her cheeky humour and a twinkle in her eye, I ask, "Where in India did you live?" Oh, she tells me, she's actually Indian Fijian, but her ancestors came from Goa, the former Portuguese colony in India. Then I ask her what she does for a crust here in Australia, not surprisingly, she teaches textile and fashion design at RMIT University part-time. That does not amaze me one bit because her sense of dress is uniquely colourful and different from the common norms of dressing. It was what drew my eyes to her when she first entered the carriage, her clothes complimenting her body shape and her tulip-shaped exotic lips beamed confidence, intelligence and an innocence that exuded her sexuality; a work of art, I thought.

Not surprisingly she asks me, "Where did you get that warm winter jacket? Its design has Indian style and type blanket motifs on it." I answer, "It's from Scotch and Soda, a Dutch fashion design house." I wanted to ask her about the little devil tattoo strategically placed in the nape of her neck, but did not yet, despite my curiosity, let no one ever tell me Indian women are demure and conservative; too many progressive, trendsetting millennial Indian women have broken that mould.

Our conversation then turned to the sameness and utter drabness of the types of clothes average Australians wear – no colour, only shades of black, grey, or white; virtually, no other colour. Commenting on my clothes, they too are different she says, certainly different than the mass-produced Asian clothes one purchases at the large ordinary clothing outlets seen in every Australian suburban shopping centre.

Again she had a good laugh while scanning at the headlines on the newspaper folded on my lap, as if she can read my mind telling me that a few Indians in Australia are like Gurpal Singh, an Indian–Australian candidate for the Liberal Party who, this morning, captured the news headlines having spouted homophobic and anti-women rhetoric as well as defending men who raped their wives, "Oh, it is so embarrassing for the Indian-Australian Community. These type of ignorant people give India a bad name and they are not even Indian values." I tell Shakti not to worry too much; Australia has no shortage of homophobes and misogynist. That very day, Gurpal Singh was dis-endorsed from the conservative Liberal Party.

Shakti tells me, she is preparing for her IELTS exam (International English Language Testing System) as she needs 80% pass marks, a must-have to gain permanent residency status in Australia. With a sigh of exasperation, she goes on to explain that she has failed to score these marks, even after sitting for it six times; she growls – 6 times at $360 a pop! This time she is worried if she does not pass, she and her husband, Vivaan, his name meaning "at the first ray of the sun" would be sent back to India. I smile and say, "Don't worry too much; if you don't pass your IELTS this time, you will not be returned to India at the first ray of the Sun! '*There are many ways to skin a cat*', or so the idiom says." Australian immigration is quite tough. I reassure her that it has nothing to do with her intelligence. 70 per cent of Australian native speakers would not pass the IELTS test, they'd all have to be sent back to the country of their ancestors if they were not the original inhabitants of this country. I hear her out, suggesting that she take some trial IELTS tests at my School of Languages where we run coaching classes for people wanting to pass their IELTS examinations. "The school is for Refugees, disadvantaged Migrants and Australians with literacy problems. We charge no fees and only accept donations," I informed her.

Wishing each other a good day, till we meet again and that would be often on the train but no more in the Quiet Carriage as we had so much to tell each other. These train journeys cemented friendships that have endured for years. In my experience, Indians make real good friends and are the type of hardworking, well-educated migrants that Australia thrives on.

Then there are my Indian students and friends in my Australian Language and Culture classes. My friend Dhruv, a young 25-year-old Indian student graduating from Monash University with a Medical degree, who privately tells me he is in trouble, somehow has very low self-esteem. Nevertheless, he, like Ajay is a very good looking, tall and handsome Indian from Punjab. He tells me he made a "white face" Australian woman pregnant four months ago. He loves her and wants to get married, quickly explaining he did not make her pregnant for permanent residency.

"Well, what is stopping you to get married or live together in a partnership," I ask. He avoided my eyes and said, "She is a prostitute working in a brothel."

"Yes, OK, but does she love you?"

"It's complicated," he replies. He had paid sex several times with the condom, but it must have ripped off and she got pregnant. At first, he denied it was his child because he had used a condom, but a DNA paternity test proved it was his child. Suddenly, Dhruv stops and says he may have gone too far in this conversation. "In India, one cannot talk about a thing like this; it brings shame. Yet, here I am talking about it with my teacher."

I encourage Dhruv to go on. He turns the conversation into some confession and says the reason why he went to the brothel was that no Australian girl wanted to be his friend. "They always kept their distance and I thought I was not handsome enough, so I worked out at the gym and created this body, hoping it would be desirable to white Australian women. That is why I went to the brothel near the hospital where I worked. I even carried my ID from the hospital thinking maybe the girls would be interested or at least be impressed to know I was a doctor."

Now the Australian woman has given birth to a boy but cannot keep it as the woman's parents have applied to the government to care for their grandson because their daughter has been identified through the courts as a drug addict. Dhruv is dismayed that the court did not give his son to him to look after. Clearly, his unnecessary shame and silence had taken its toll and he needed professional help beyond that, which I was able to provide.

I introduced Dhruv to an Indian social worker and psychologist. Dhruv's self-esteem needed work, yet he was an Adonis, but his low self-worth and inferiority complex of being Indian in a white world contributed to this. He did not have any friends in the Indian community because he felt they were judging him, making him feel that he was not good enough and he should not do all this body-work because people might think he was Gay. The truth was that Dhruv did meet many Gay men who worked out at the Gym. They became his friends and accepted him for what he was without any prejudice or judgments. They even tried to introduce him to the many girl-friends gay men are famous for having, women as their best friends.

CHAPTER 3

THE LONGING OF OUR SOULS IS ALWAYS THE LONGING OF A LOVER

We're on the plane, at last. The purpose of our travel to India is twofold – one, to attend the Hindu wedding of Ajay's brother, Jag; and second, to explore and observe the ancient wisdom and culture of India in the way ordinary people live and reflect that in their lives ignoring the hubris of mainstream media and the often biased opinions of academics, politicians, priests and tourist brochures.

Staring out of an Airbus 380 window ten kilometres above the Indian Ocean looking at innumerable stars decorating the universe is an exhilarating buoyant experience while listening to Holst's Planets on earphones. I wondered if other beings on the stars could see the earth as I saw them, activating a train of thoughts about the riddle and mysteriousness of existence. It provoked a sense of cosmic loneliness, almost sadness, as I missed sharing these thoughts with my loved ones and friends who are no longer present in the body; a melancholic mood overtook me.

On occasions like these, my memory temporarily reverts to 1960, when travelling on a KLM Constellation, before the jet age, flying to The Netherlands was a three-and-a-half days'

A vegan meal with Ajay, my Australian-Indian travelling companion before boarding the Airbus A380 flying from Melbourne to India.

journey, with stopovers in Hollandia, Dutch New Guinea on to Manila, Karachi, Beirut, Rome, Frankfurt and finally Amsterdam. Travel in those days was a prestigious lifetime event. For the occasion, my parents gave me a quality, light wool, three-piece suit and shoes, shirts, ties and socks, all Australian made and designed. Nothing in the way of clothes and shoes and the spinning of high-quality wool happens in Australia today, we've become the nation of the great derivative. Everybody in those long-ago days dressed well, especially when travelling on an ocean liner or on an aeroplane. Mum included two non-iron shirts and underwear changes for the three-day journey including soap and male fragrance, I think it was *Tabac* fragrance. To this day I find this fragrance comforting. On all our stops we would wash or shower, dine in the finest hotels for a three-course dinner sitting, a good way to meet classy fellow travellers. The in-between meals on the plane were not a plastic cutlery spoon, plate and cup affair with mass-produced chemically addicted and preserved food affairs. No, everything was fresh and there was room to stretch my long legs. In those days, you were called by your first name, at least I was because I suppose I was just a teenager with good cultural tastes. I snapped out of my nostalgic moment, sad to realise I was now on a type of glorified flying cattle truck smelling of stale urine sitting amongst some people who appeared to be incontinent.

Sitting next to me were my two travelling companions, Darius and Ajay, both fun-loving and highly vibrational beings having an interest in all beautiful things. Ajay gave me a friendly push saying stop dreaming and handed me the menu. It was time to order our Vegan meals. It was Ajay who first awakened my interest in India. He is an easy-going, fun-loving and a conscientious friend, highly intelligent, evident by his intriguing conversations above the banally superfluous. His spirituality was heightened by the appeal of his childhood memories when he wanted to reclaim his life force, which he had at the beginning of his youth. Consequently, he had recently taken up the study of philosophy and was returning to his spiritual roots after experimenting with the hedonistic forays of a young man's life where he encountered his vexation of spirit and discovered all was vanity. To his friends, it seemed his personality might be changing from phlegmatic to more of a melancholic.

Ajay is an Indian name for a handsome, invincible man. He is determined, smart and gifted with the ability to see into the other souls around him.

Darius, on the other hand, is a spiritual, sensual, fun-loving and a caring friend who loves health and fitness, especially the body-mind experience and anything to do with the mystery of consciousness. Even though he is a fitness and fashion model, he remains humble and in touch with his roots encouraging people out of their dysfunctionality using himself as an example. He has all the traits of a true Sanguine personality and makes friends easily. In his life, there always seems to be the pull between the contemplative life of the spirit and the life of the flesh: envied by others, he thrives on compliments. He is not the smartest but pretty smart. He can be manipulative to get his way and his sensuality is far beyond those who have lived many lifetimes. Everyone needs a Darius, a good lover that cares. His kindness combined with a bit of flirting and salaciousness has a place in this world. Like Ajay, he is gifted; he knows your thoughts before you do, at times, unpredictable and relentless. His name says it all "He who holds firm to good".

Darius' upbringing and values reflect the most perfect qualities of Australia's multiculturalism, '*live and let live with respect*'. His ancestors, according to these advertised DNA tests, are Dutch, Persian and Jewish, hence, the name Darius after the Persian Zoroastrian King Darius.

Ajay, Darius and I have been more than close friends, always doing something nice for each other even if it were small gestures, asking good questions, especially when we vented and needed a good listener. We got to know each other through struggles and challenges. Paying attention and maintaining eye contact without interrupting, and there was and is always a high level of emotional intimacy – Non-*heteronormative*, cultural expressions transcending matters of sexual orientation. Our friendship can best be described as a non-sexual *bromance relationship*. It can have some nice tints of romance, you might give a flower, some male fragrance, a box of high-quality Belgian chocolates. It is honest conversations about everything; it is a very close friendship between male friends that are not into brutish banter or competitive braggadocio of the *bogan* type of dysfunctional males such as many of the Australian AFL, NRL players who are constantly in the news for all the wrong reasons.

Ajay and Darius have two things in common; they don't know this because they haven't known about this common link. This commonness will be revealed in our journey to India, sitting on this plane in the present. Ajay had been telling me about his meditation and lifestyle changes so he could become close to the Master and he too could become God, cheekily prompting me to say, "But you are already a God." Walking past my Australian wattle tree growing in my front garden, he stopped to squeeze sapping the leaves explaining that he wanted us to meditate together. Apparently, the sap of the leaves produces DMT, a hallucinogenic tryptamine drug that occurs naturally in certain types of wattle tree; when taken, it produces an intensely visual, auditory and sensual hallucinating experience. Saying his meditation practice was like that and he wanted me to experience with him our minds bodies and psyches so that they would become one. He told me he saw angels and heard beautiful ethereal music when he meditated with his Indian-Canadian friend, a Bollywood film producer.

A few days after Ajay told me about the DMT hallucinations, Darius too wanted me to try a Zoroastrian drink called

Hauma, mixed with plant milk. Of all other intoxicants, it was mind-altering, accompanying deep insights and gladding truth. He told me I should drink it as Zoroastrian poets, writers and lovers did it to increase their power of expression and visionary imagination and have communion with the divine. Darius said this could be a connection between the unseen and the seen, between the soul and the body. Then, he undid all he said by giving a mischievous wink.

When travelling, one of the things I find entertaining is observing people, and yet, sometimes it is a cause of annoyance and aggravation, such as right now when the *bogan* Australian guy and his woman sitting behind us rest their ugly bare feet over the top of our seats. Overhearing and observing them I am sure they suffer from BPD, a borderline personality disorder. Why do airline companies allow the lowest common denominator with behavioural problems to travel? Oh, there is a very large person wearing black tights about three sizes too small and another wearing thongs on their bare feet! Then, I hear another *bogan* yelling out to the stewardesses, "Hey love, when are you serving the grog", *is there no civility anymore*, my mind questions. We called this person 'Mate' because every second word he was using was "mate" ad infinitum, calling out to the stewards, "hey mate", thanks matey and turning to us asked, "Where are you mates from, you don't look *Stralain* like me, mate, I am from Oz." It is moments like these when one is embarrassed to be an Australian and you'd wish the ground would open up and swallow the 'matey types'. "Good on you mate," Darius said we can be mates only if you keep your feet to yourself instead of putting them over the top of our seats, above our heads. "Okay mate, sorry mate."

Darius and I Googled much prior before going to India and consulted the Lonely Planet and Baedeker tourists guides, but none of these would tell us about the hearts, body, mind and spirit of the Indian people. The guides give the impression that India is only a museum of antiquities and art. However, to us, to love and understand the Indian people, they are more important than the land.

What about the norms and values of the Indian people, what are the important things? Well, Ajay says there are such a variety of value systems set by parents, religion, peer groups and educational systems. On a personal level, you should be true to your own values. Just then, Ajay gently reprimands Darius for winking at two older Indian women sitting across our aisle, they gave such a look of disapproval; obviously, they were thinking that any guy that smiles, talks or winks at them immediately thinks they're getting hit on; but young Indian women in Australia enjoy a nice smile and a wink from attractive men. A lot of the things I hear about how I should behave in India seem to be manufactured from the factory of bias and ignorance. *Joie de vie*

The apartment looked like Art Deco with a slash of Indianese, we liked this kind of Indian chic.

CHAPTER 4

IT FELT SPECIAL AND AWESOME BEING GREETED BY SUCH A MIX OF NOVELTY AND CURIOSITY THAT MADE THIS ARRIVAL IN INDIA SO NICE

It is not an insignificant moment to touch down in the world's largest fully functioning democracy, the birthplace of one of the most ancient and spiritual nations on planet earth where 1.339 billion people live, love and have their being. I was excited by the possibilities of an expansion of my consciousness. "This India is really something," Darius exclaimed as the gorgeous glamour of Indian images of colour, sound and taste came to life as soon as we stepped foot on Indian soil. There was nothing cheap or shabby about the ultra-modern and efficient Indira Gandhi International Airport in New Delhi.

Gurinder, a Sikh and fellow passenger on the flight from Dubai told us about the Indian push factor – when queuing, do not leave a space longer than your arm or someone will butt in; you should only leave a space from your elbow to your fingertip. He then smiled and reminded us that personal space in India is of absolutely no consequence as it is in the west. Indians see nothing disrespectful or invasive in jostling each other around. In the Netherlands or Australia, we find this behaviour rude and inconsiderate, but this kind of aggressive assertiveness is part of the Indian ethos. Indians always have to compete for any space. Personal space, I discovered, is not only defined in physical terms, but Indians are also natural intruders into each other's lives. They see nothing wrong with developing intimacy with another person, even total strangers. They easily picked up conversations with us everywhere even standing in the Visa checking queue.

A Mediterranean looking man, tall, well-built, around 25 years old, well-spoken, looking not unlike Ajay standing in front of me, while waiting to have my Electronic Visa validated, smiled and said, "Allow me to welcome you to India. My name is *Ampilos Dionysos,*" graciously presenting his business card and inviting us anytime we were in India for tea and group discussions about philosophy, religion, literature or poetry. He said his aim was to fuse Christ and Dionysus and for us to discover the secret impulses of antiquity and the tools for redemption and ecstasy, quickly adding that he knew who I was as he had a dream about Darius, Ajay and me. I could not say much except smile and accept his visitor's card. He quickly continued his spiel saying the Greek God Dionysus who through orgiastic rites became the Indian Lord Shiva. *Ampilos* said his teachings would re-establish and practice alternative visions of reality with the purpose of creating a better future for the individual, and that he was looking to invite westerners to his *sacred grove,* for a price, especially northern Europeans with blue eyes, and who were enlightened liberal progressive Christians opposite to the cruel American Trump-loving Evangelical or conservative fundamentalists types.

At this stage, my bullshit radar was on full alert in detecting charmers and charlatans mystic and scholars, yet realizing that to see beauty, I had to allow myself to be touched by things and people and not be too dismissive. Consequently, I gave

Ampilos a polite affiliate smile, the type indicating a social and spiritual connection, and thanked him. He awakened my curiosity enough for me to promise we would visit his *sacred grove* whilst in India.

After a ten-minute interaction with customs, a young boy walked towards us with a serving tray of hot coffees beaming with a "welcome to India". What should we do, accept it? What was in the coffee? How much would we be charged? He was so friendly. I profusely thanked him and said I could not accept the coffee using the excuse of a weak stomach. Then, Ajay smiled and called out to drink. He had already paid the young boy as a gesture of surprise and welcome. While sipping the very sweet coffees, a Yogi was practising his Yoga moves stretching and breathing, doing a handstand and staying there for three minutes defying gravity, his age about 90 years, and fit. Once done, he gave us a welcome greeting with a great smile containing much kindness. He still had all his white sparkling teeth. *Must be his vegan diet*, a fleeting thought impressed.

Reflecting and waiting for Darshan and Jag, Ajay's father and brother to pick us up, the last thirty minutes since we landed, we had already experienced delightful surprises, secrets and revelations. When they arrived, Darius and I stood at a distance respecting the reconnection of family. Sometimes that can be emotional and people need space. Not that there was too much personal space, constantly I reminded myself that we were now in the most densely populated country in the world and in the company of stimulating and interesting people. Yet, it was so amazing that we got out of the airport so quickly. Indians are experienced people movers and obviously people makers. It felt special and awesome being greeted by that mix of novelty and curiosity.

Piling into the family car with our minimal luggage, thank goodness we travel light, just one small bag each, nothing more, it beats me why so many tourists deliberately burden themselves with so much baggage, "both physically and mentally", Ajay was quick to observe. Everything I needed, fitted in my small backpack – six pairs of jogs, three pairs of socks, toiletry bag containing the essentials, headache and Diarize tablets just in case I would suffer dehydration, toothbrush, deodorant stick, skin moisturizer, liquid soap, shampoo all in very small containers and a bottle of expensive male fragrance, worn to make an impression, people remember fragrances and it "attracts people like bees, and people remember you," Darius mused. Then there were the scientifically woven, quick-drying, self-cleaning and all-absorbent travel towels, two pair of long trousers, three T-shirts, one woollen jumper and our IPads and smartphones. Jag had organised our Indian prepaid sim cards for 1500 rupees per month, unlimited data with the speed and reliability one can only dream of in Australia. Off we rode to Cyber City, the Silicon Valley area of India, just outside of New Delhi, 20 km from the airport yet it only took 15 minutes to get there. After all, it was 2 am on 11 October 2018. The roads were well made, smooth and clean. I noticed paid women sweeping the streets and footpaths.

From the outside, Jag's apartment, built in the 1990s, looked like Art Deco style with a slash of Indianese architecture. We liked this Indian chic, and we were up for a new experience of drinking genuine Chai Latte Tea. Darshan boiled the water, threw in three sticks of cinnamon, fennel seeds, fresh ginger and black peppercorns, coriander seeds and star anise sweetened with honey. We took part in the ritual of sipping this heavenly tea before sleep. The beds in the apartments were king size. Many Indian people, particularly Sikhs, are tall people. Darius and I slept in one of these, Ajay and Jag in another, and Darshan in a single bed. I discovered it was not uncommon that even modern Indian families often sleep in one large bed together. The night was hot and we just needed a black silk sheet with a colonial type Indian ceiling fan softly humming over our languorous bodies, momentarily drifting into the romantic period of the British Raj.

Early in the morning, our Indian host did meditation. After that, we exercised by running a few times around the block. It was still hot but not humid or a debilitating heat, the type that sucks out energy. The streets were already busy, people walking or speeding on their moped, scooters and bicycles. On our run, we met the local street cleaning brigade, a roaming mother pig and piglets scavenging and eating anything organic and leftover food from people's breakfast. The streets were spotlessly clean. Darius leading the charge, manoeuvring and avoiding collisions between good looking cows and speeding mopeds. The fresh fragrance of red and white frangipanis, with varieties of colourful Bougainvillea, wafting exotic aromas throughout the neighbourhood. Street vendors had already set up their colourful, fresh fruits and vegetable stands. I pinched myself; I was in India or in Ocean Grove Victoria.

Even if I say so, Darius has a truly healthy and fit body, the type that people would turn their heads for. That morning he was wearing a white muscle T-shirt and athletic lycra running shorts. We stopped at one of the attractive juice making carts for a fresh cantaloupe drink mixed with very sweet Indian oranges. The young woman mixing the juice asked if his biceps were real, wanting to apply her squeeze test on his biceps. Another young man wanted to know about his vegan diet and how many push-ups he could do. True to form, Indian curiosity about us white faces came to the fore and they were surprised to know we were vegan. Their notion of western people was that they were all flesh eaters and drenched themselves with alcohol and had little respect for body, mind and spirit. Explanations ensued and hopefully, we broke their stereotypes of western white faces – not all are dead flesh eaters and alcoholics.

However, I have to admit that we did later drink milk and ate yoghurt and the traditional three varieties of Lassie, salty, sweet, mango blended with Indian spices and a variety of fruit. The rationale used by me to begin to drink milk was that unlike Australia, Indian Desi calves are not taken away from their mother and they are not killed or bred for white veal. My conscience was soothed that the milk I would drink came from happy mum cows and their calves.

That afternoon we caught up with Tey, a Hindu Priest whom Darius met at a spiritual vegan health and fitness retreat in Australia. Tey also lived around Cyber City and had a smallish type marble temple serving spiritual food and refreshing drinks and the aroma of glorious incense sticks. At the temple, Tey enjoyed legal cannabis to be in touch with Krishna, one of the Avatars of the God Vishnu. We did try an infused drink that contains bhang, a liquid derivative of cannabis, which has an effect similar to other eaten forms of cannabis. It is legal in many parts of India and mainly sold during Holi, the festival of love, when pakoras containing bhang are also sometimes eaten; something like the coffee shops of Amsterdam with which I was familiar, here they have licensed bhang shops. Perfectly rested, we were ready the next day for 12 hours on the Grand Trunk Road, deep into Punjab. We had only been in India for a few hours and yet a web of intrigue, love and enlightenment was being spun. Here we were looking at the world as though one had never seen it before. Stripped of familiar connotations for me, it was a pure perception, a fresh vision.

CHAPTER 5

A PERSONAGE OF ZENITH BEAUTY AND PERFECTION, AN AVATAR I THOUGHT

The world is made up of dreams, I mused, sitting alone on the kerbside, taking in the ambience of old Amritsar oozing its other-worldliness of character and ambience with its stunning old-style colonial architecture reminiscent of the British Raj period, more like a movie set than reality, although it was reality, not a movie set. The kerbside observations and dreaming aroused my curiosity no doubt spurned on by the dazzling street bazaars full of euphonic sounds, colourful saris and kurtas, euphoric aromas and intoxicating incense and the beautiful people had a mesmerizing effect on all my senses and everything, realising that for everything there is always something else.

This other-worldliness contrasted sharply with Punjabi millennials zooming, crisscrossing about on their mopeds wearing tight jeans, leggings and T-shirts emblazoned with clichéd western slogans and motifs. Clutching Apples and Galaxies as though they're newly evolved appendages on their youthful bodies. To my western mind, there appeared to be mass traffic anarchy on the roads, yet there was calm. Despite witnessing so many near misses, aggressiveness and road rage

He said, "I saw you gently stroke my sacred cow."

does not prevail. The main game for each moped, bicycle, horse cart, truck, car and pedestrian, is to avoid collisions, hurt and damage and to arrive alive in one piece, just like everywhere else in the world.

My dreamy chai (tea) intoxicated mind slowly drifted into a state of Déjà vu just when a personage of zenith beauty and perfection plops himself next to me on the kerbside; simultaneously touching gently on my shoulder and greeting in a soft but strong attractive voice, "hallo Keith, welcome to Amritsar." Astonishment populates my mind, how does he know my name amongst the hundreds of thousands of Amritsar denizens. Before saying his name, I knew intuitively his name was Krishna and greeted him, "Hi Krishna, you've arrived." He looked splendidly familiar, an image one never forgets. Was the ancient city of Amritsar releasing its spirits and secrets momentarily? I thought he might have been an Avatar because he had the glow of such ethereal light about him or maybe I had had too much Bodhi Chai (tea); or had I been here before in a previous life? How long has this encounter been lying latent in my sub-consciousness, who can tell?

Krishna explained that he saw me talking to his favourite sacred Desi cow outside the *Alexander Lassi* bar just across the gym where he was having a workout when he met Darius who told Krishna who I was. "I knew you were the only whiteface sitting here on the kerb." I have to admit that when I heard my name called, it felt like a casual caress in an exotic place.

All this excitement of meeting new invigorating personages stimulated our appetites, especially after gym exercise and workouts. We offered to "shout" Krishna lunch at a nearby Sattvic Restaurant. He didn't understand Australian English and told us that we don't need to shout, we can eat in quietness. Darius advised me to speak British English, not Australian English because the Indians do not understand Australian idioms. So, we rephrased it and explained that shouting someone lunch means to treat them to lunch, "You'll be our guest."

During lunch, our curiosity aroused about Pehelwani wrestlers because Krishna was a prime example of a person glowing in excellent health through practising the 3000-year-old health and diet practices contained in the *Vedic Ayurveda,* life oracles advocating balancing mind, body and spirit through a vegetarian diet, exercise and good interpersonal relationships.

Pehelwani wrestlers such as Krishna shun all foods that cause lethargy, no sugary starchy foods or alcohol because as Krishna believes, they cause degeneration of the body and mind telling that the millennia-old *Sattvic* diet of freshly grown nuts, fruits, legumes, vegetables, herbs and plants is the best for him, not the manufactured packet foods as sold in western countries. Krishna compares himself with Ajay's balanced and aesthetically pleasing body. Then, being very serious, he says that so many westerners use protein supplements, cheekily squeezing Darius's and Ajay's biceps and feeling the firmness of their chest. "Nothing flabby," he laughs, adding, "these are made from steroids and protein supplements." We smile wryly and exclaim, "No! And no!"

Krishna's inspiration came from Vedic archetypes such as *Hanuman* who lived near Amritsar and led a disciplined lifestyle. Krishna saw him as the patron god of Indian martial arts symbolizing the human excellence of self-control and respect, virtues worth striving for.

Perfection, one of his virtues serves every human endeavour such as the arts, science and aesthetics. All of these are stimuli to reach the reality of dreams. We told him that this is one of the reasons for our visit to India, in our search of perception that would give us a fresh vision of India, seeing the world as we had never seen it before. Krishna made us see, for the first time that in innocence abides a lot of love. We in the west are too focused on *reason,* of course, we agree that 'reason' is a triumph of human evolution, although we cast doubt on this when one considers the current crop of world leaders and climate change deniers. I don't think 'reason' should overstep its boundaries and we must not allow it to overtake love, passion and enthusiasm, spirituality and human beauty in all its forms and character. Therefore, 'reason' must be kept in check or it could destroy our empathy, altruism, our vision and dreams. I frequently replace reason with consequences: what are the consequences if I move to a healthy and fit lifestyle?

Krishna asked why we westerners did not feel uncomfortable him touching our bodies and leaning on us. He had previously observed uptight western men and boys, noticing that many were struggling with feelings of emptiness, not getting much affection, not being comfortable with themselves, leading to aggression and using mind-altering substances all because of having been deprived of reassuring gentle platonic touches probably imposed on them by generations of puritanical mistrust. He leans on Darius for a few minutes and says he often holds his friends' hands or sit close together; it's just such a natural thing to do by choice. Ajay, an Indian himself, agrees and says the mental health of men in Australia is very poor and Australia has one of the highest rates of male suicides and very high domestic violence and divorces for those married. Echoes of a conversation we had with Gurinder, an anthropologist when he said that "Indians are natural intruders into each other's lives, they see nothing wrong with developing intimacy with another person, even total strangers. They easily pick up conversations and don't waste any time. They give much and ask for an equal portion back; this is often misunderstood by westerners."

A Déjà vu kind of trance took over again and I was transported to another time that Krishna had ignited when earlier he provided a few sentences while casually saying that the sweet Lassi and sour yoghurt I was having was a leftover from the Greek soldiers of Alexander the Great. I was slow to catch on, the penny did not drop until the chatting was over some more Bodhi Chai (tea). The waiters had obviously been eavesdropping and spontaneously joined us in the conversation, enthusiastically telling us about their recent DNA tests revealing that some of the Punjabis had 26% and an average of 15% DNA from Aryan and Greek ancestors. I could see this just by looking at different races in India and particularly the Indian Punjabis being tall and almost fair-skinned, a handsome race of people.

One of the waiters with a long name of *Chandragupta,* named after the King who found the first Indian Empire tells me to just call him Chandry. He says that not very far from here, in 326BCE, along the formidable mighty *Beas river,* Alexander's march was stopped from entering further into Punjab. On the banks of the Beas River, the Greek troops defied Alexander's order to cross over and continued their conquest of India. However, they suffered a severe blow inflicted by the valiant Indian soldiers of *King Porus* of Punjab and his Warrior Elephants including thousands of well-trained Pehelwani wrestlers such as Krishna, "Indian Soldiers of great valour," Chandry said. "The Indians had the hand in negotiating peace after some sixty-thousand Alexander's soldiers settled in Punjab near the *Amritsar-Taren Taren Belt* area." Darius who just could not stop himself surmised that Alexander's soldiers who stayed behind procreated as fiercely as they had fought and we can see the results all-round Punjab, a northern state of India. Chandry offered to show us more remnants, so we planned to visit some of the remnants of the influenced Punjabi-Greco Culture.

I felt mentally well-satisfied and began to wane, a sign I needed some quiet time after many hours of chatting. Darius and Krishna continued chatting with great animation about finding equilibrium through body, mind and spirit and the constant exploration of ourselves. We had aroused each other's admiration. It was evident that Krishna loved us with brotherly love. We would love *Agape* style, unconditionally and inclusively. Krishna had become part of our extended family, the Indian way.

We are continents apart yet the real beauty of Krishna still nourishes and inspires us with such qualities as intelligence, ability to love, sincerity, intellectual truth and power, philosophy and literature.

Jewellery in India denotes culture and spirituality. Indian men too wear muscular jewellery, which acts as an agent of personality.

CHAPTER 6

JEWELLERY

"With undivided emotion, Joyita showed the many pieces of popular Indian jewellery assisted by Das Das who was also gifted with the ability to see into the souls around him and able to sense his clients' character and destiny"

Joyita, our transgender jewellery designer took us into her atelier, a converted Hamman (Ancient Arab Bathhouse) into an artist colony for jewellers, fashion designers, sculptors, artistic painters, musicians; wandering through the old Hammas. The stimulating forces of thought and creative ideas entered my consciousness, no doubt triggered by the metaphysical sweetness of wafting hemp fumes. I had read somewhere that writers, actors and painters stimulated new thoughts and ideas that advanced society; now I know that is true. Perhaps the ultimate measure in the world is not about truth but about creating beauty.

Joyita's male co-designer, Das Das is a specialist stylist in personalising and creating jewellery to bring out our best body features such as face, neck, ears, nose, legs, toes and fingers, the most desirable feature being your personality. He gets close to you so he gets to know our instincts, what works best. He tells us that in most cultures, jewellery is worn to adorn to enhance every part of the body from hairpins to toe rings, genital and tongue piercing often worn as objects d'art by individuals.

Curiosity satisfied over Arabic coffee and conversations, Joyita explained the here, whys and wherefores of Indians' excessive preoccupation with gold, diamonds and precious stones. Jewellery denotes everything about Indian lives, wealth and security. It is the favourite object used in denoting culture, sexuality and spirituality. It has strong ties to Animism, (from the Latin anima meaning breath, spirit and life) the spiritual belief that objects such as jewellery possess a distinct spiritual essence, almost a type of soul with its own sentience evident from how much value jewellery holds for humans. Darius pulled out a Saint Christopher medal that he carried in his pocket, a gift from his grandmother to ward off evil spirits, and ensures safety. He kisses the medal as though power and security radiate from it.

Das Das is more articulate in describing personal jewellery and states the unsaid but obvious. Jewellery is sexy, it's innuendo, it says things that would be impolite or crass to communicate with words; this too partly explains the fascination with jewellery, it always makes us more conscious of our body. It sort of is a polymorphism. We behave differently when we don't wear jewellery feeling so metaphysical, relating to things that are thought to exist but that cannot be seen, like spiritually feeling alone and naked like true animist, when we don't wear it. Darius and his Saint Christopher medal and his pierced tongue feels venerable and naked without wearing this kind of jewellery.

So what does it all mean, this jewellery, what does it symbolize? With undivided emotion, Joyita showed the many pieces of popular Indian jewellery assisted by Das Das who was also gifted with the ability to see into the souls around him and able to sense his clients' character and destiny. Here he showcases an elaborate ear-cuff worn by Hindu Scholar priest showing off his extraordinary jewellery-making skills, him being the expert in male jewellery. Indian-specific jewellery is not only attractive but has scientific connotations in Ayurvedic literature.

"Take the nose ring," he says, *"the nose ring* is the most seductive jewel piece without which a married woman's make up is incomplete. Ayurveda science considers women having pierced noses experience less pain in childbirth and it prevents her from being hypnotized by other men, not her husband because of the nose ring's power to control the brain wavelengths."

The *Earrings* are not only sexy but they are also essential: many believe that evil spirits enter the body through any of its seven male and eight for female openings. Ear decorations are a microcosm of the entire body having nerves that connect cervix, brain and kidney. Darius, forever verbalizing the obvious says, "That explains why lovers nibble the ear lobes whispering sweet nothings." It is good for the health of kidney and bladders and a good stimulation of the ear lobes is good for female conception.

Necklaces worn near the heart control the emotions and are protective against hypnotizing and evil charms against virtuous maidens and young men. They strengthen one's love for their partners, but that doesn't explain Ajay's $5000 golden male necklace, he does not have a partner. Wearing a necklace of stones is believed to bind ourselves, to join in with eternal powers bringing good luck and ward off evil eyes.

Bangles are worn by most Indian males and females. All can afford them made from precious metals or wood. A women's beauty is incomplete without this ornament. The sound of a women's bangle expresses her presence and her wish to gain attention. Scientifically, bangles increase blood circulation and channelize the energy passing through the outer skin, and of course, the euro-phonic sounds of tinkling are assuring to the Indian soul. Ajay's attention focuses on Joyita's bangles and says he wants some bangles like those, for his mother Amara, and for Misha, his future sister-in-law as well as for Jag. Every bracelet or bangle had its own love and cultural story to tell. Besides enhancing the beauty and sensuality of Indian women and men, it is also a matter of great security; you can always sell gold for a rainy day. Ajay bought so many gold bangles, he said women love them as they have immense romantic and amorous connotations; the jingle bell sound expresses her presence and her wish to gain attention, "Jewelled bangles make us more attractive and desirable and so we get noticed," Joyita says.

Aren't all humans peacocks? It is the soul that adds colour to our lives. She looks at Ajay, smiles and says, "You're looking for a wife. I have a piece of jewellery in the form of a scarf bedecked with some precious stones. Put some vermillion on it and all you do is take the opportunity when you're at a festival such as Diwali, you place this vermilion scarf on a chosen girl's heads. Sometimes a betrothal ceremony takes place very quickly, even before proper marriage is solemnized.

Mangalsutra, a gift from the bridegroom to the bride during the wedding is worn by the married woman symbolizing feelings of love and commitment between the married couple. The jewellery chakra is visualized by two petals, half male and half female where the androgynous deity Ardhanarishvara resides. It symbolizes the meeting of the male and female elements in nature at both the physical and mental level. *Wearing* a ring on the fourth finger from the thumb is directly connected to the nerve passing through this finger to the brain neuron cells and is connected to the heart, controlling the wearer's emotions. Nowadays, rings of various stones are worn by women for various health benefits.

In India, male-dominated traditions have been maintained throughout the Vedic classical, medieval and modern Hinduism;

the paradigms in myth, rituals, doctrines and symbols are masculine. There is a Goddess tradition too and is impacting the lives of modern Indian women.

Das Das offers to create a special piece of jewellery for Darius and suggests a stunning ear cuff for him called a *Bhikbali,* an ornament initially worn by Brahmin scholars as a symbol of knowledge and intelligence. Nowadays, *Bhikbali* has become a symbol of pride and prestige.

Historical evidence is produced by Das Das showing that men in many parts of India mostly dressed only the lower half of their bodies in clothes and the upper part of their body was covered by gold and precious stones, jewellery as illustrated by the pictures in Kamasurta. Old carvings and ancient art show the same. The tantric jewellery and cultural traditions of 5000 years ago, these lifestyles are now returning to modern India and made popular all over the world.

Joyita again emphasizes that the sacred and symbolic jewellery impacts the lives of Indian men as it harnesses the power of spiritual symbols and put emphasis on their masculinity, vitality and love. The role of male jewellery is 'to be noticed'; they want to be in the centre of attention. Leather cuffs braided or solid, they wear with T-shirts and jeans; it gives a rugged or masculine look.

Throughout all this, Ajay had been quiet and he was the reason for our stopover in Dubai – the purchase of wedding gold and jewellery. Ajay looked the most exotic out of us three presenting like a handsome Indian prince. His physique was muscular as he had been working out extra hard for the wedding. He had promised his older brother Jag to be a desirable temple of holiness, primarily to attract the right young female for him to marry. The friendly but persistent urging from his parents and aunties and uncles who urged him to get hitched, the sooner the better, he was already getting too old they thought, even if only a 28 years young man. Consequently, he was working on the 'status stakes', all-important for Indian families especially when arranging marriages for their children. Ajay was deliberately flaunting and signalling that he was good and ready, perfect husband material. He had just purchased a four-bedroom house in Melbourne as soon as he graduated with a Bachelor of Education, an all-impressive status.

The time of drinking coffee was up and now we were off to Joyita's gold shop where Ajay was going to part with some serious money. Here we were witness to Ajay, brilliant at haggling tactics showing no emotion or surprise; just one big haggling poker face. That is the reason why he was so quiet at the coffee table. He just listened but not a word; he was working out a strategy. We knew the price of gold was set internationally and there could be no discounts on that, but he knew he could haggle about the manufacturing cost of the jewellery, which was usually locally made. Before we left, we had to do some more shopping for perfume, scents and incense, and material for henna art to decorate the bride with.

CHAPTER 7

YOU ARE WHAT YOU ARE, DEAR

In India, the fantastic and the rich combine. It is here where one sees deep into the human heart and soul because everything is right up close into your face.

One could never miss seeing them, these unique extraordinary group of women covered in their multi-coloured designer Temple Saris projecting an exuberant vibrancy enhanced by shining jewellery and conspicuous make-up. They presented as a sort of welcoming troupe spread out amongst the two large toll gates on the Grand Trunk Road on our way to Jalandhar.

During his meditation and dreaming, Darius had seen these young women and pretty looking men before, maybe from a previous life. Here they were again the same people meeting him once more, this time on a 2000-year-old road. They did not fail to raise our curiosity; intriguing us with their slender figures, belly belts, naths aka nose rings, Tikas and bejewelled golden Mangalsutras, spectacles to behold. They were a walking living cultural India, all attached in one human body.

Our car windows were down absorbing all the sounds and 'smells' of India including the headache-causing diesel exhaust fumes. A charming young man showed his image through the

The Hijras, of India, are one of the most recognized and socially accepted groups of third genders. Many Indians believe they have been reincarnated into Hijras; this does not mean that they have an easy life, Darius said, because some bigoted and nasty Indians like their equals in Australia are totally ignorant of the third sex.

open window saying, "Here I am; my name is Kaif and this is my friend Sandhya. Where are you from? You look European." If the first impression is a lasting expression, one couldn't help but admire the smiling friendliness of the Hijras. Sandhya was most attractive in terms of having a radiant personality, and her dress was definitely a sort of Indian chic, gracefully moving, flitting around from car to car, asking for alms and dispensing blessings when a money gift is made. In Australia, transgender people and drag queens often look so much more feminine than the average Australian woman, but then Darius thought that transgender women are never average, certainly not the Hijra people of India. Kaif looked more like a pretty young man; he would not have liked that as no doubt he was trying hard to create a feminine look, we learnt later he was transsexual, but to us, he looked and presented like a late teenager, worldly-wise sparkly, very winsome and respectful.

Ajay, noticing our curiosity and desire for new experiences, quickly responded with a matter of fact expression, almost in a curt tone, giving an explanation about these women being transgender, "They are the third sex in India," he said. I equated this third sex with the concept of the third eye. My mind flashed back when Darshan told me, back in Australia during his attendance at my English class that the third eye in the forehead is the eye of insights leading to inner realms and spaces of higher consciousness. Darius too recalled his studies about the *pineal gland,* also being referred to as the third eye. The pineal gland, he said is the gland that looks like a pine cone that releases a lot of hormones such as melatonin and is stimulated by sunlight and a kiss on the forehead. Developing this third eye is essential for health; that is why Sandhya and Kaif kissed us on the forehead, I figured. Darius himself and other friends would often kiss me on the forehead when he awakened me sort of like Saint Paul's holy Christian kiss on the forehead. These special third eye kisses actually help the pineal gland releasing the amino acids pinealocyte and tryptophan, which regulate our circadian rhythm.

Not being wholly ignorant of the ancient Vedic books and ancient Indian history, recognizing the third sex as being perfectly normal, and of late, but far too late, modern western science also seems to support this sexual dimorphism through the science of understanding sex chromosomes. It dawned on us that these ancient Indian cultures including the Mahu of Hawaii and the Dineh Indians in the US acknowledge four genders - feminine women, masculine women, famine men, and masculine men. The term third gender is prevalent and accepted in all cultures except in the West where misinformed moralist and anti-science conservatives cause much grief for people who are different.

The Hijras of India are one of the most recognized and socially accepted groups of third genders. Many Indians believe they have been reincarnated into Hijras this does not mean that they have an easy life, Darius said, because some bigoted and nasty Indians, like their equals in Australia, are totally ignorant of the third sex.

However, the arch of justice and righteousness is bending towards the Hijras. On the very day, we met our Hijra friends, a case was presented before the Supreme Court of India where a transgender Hijra wanted to marry a man. The Court heard the case and Judge GR Swaminathan said that the authorities were wrong in having referred to past judgments of the Indian Supreme Court. The judge declared that the 'personhood' of transgender persons has been recognized under the Indian constitution and trans-genders were free to marry. This ruling will make it easier for trans-brides and grooms alike in India to get married without discrimination. The court asked the registrar to register a marriage between the groom and his trans-woman partner, saying that the words bride in the Hindu Marriage Act includes transsexuals too.

Suddenly, we were falling into another world where the past turned up in front of us as it so often happens in India. "But why are you moving around all the cars and trucks here at the Toll Gate," I asked. Sandhya answered quickly, "We're earning our living by blessing people with a promise of good fortune and healthy life." Later, for a fee, she would offer a prophecy about our lives and a revelation of who we were in our previous past lives.

Darius was intrigued enough by them to ask Sandhya and Kaif out for lunch at the Haveli Restaurant in Jalandhar, 10 minutes away. They hopped in the back of the car and we drove off. Looking at them and sitting next to them in the car, I could not help but sing:

"I am what I am
I don't want praise, I don't want pity
I bang my own drum
Some think its noise, I think it's pretty
And so what if I love each sparkle and each bangle.
Why not try to see things from a different angle
Your life is a sham
Till you can shout out
I am what I am."

Lyrics written by John Barrowman, song composed by Jerry Herman.

I knew from ancient times that the Hijras were bestowed with spiritual gifts including prophecy, all special talents and insights. Our curiosity got the better, paying 400 rupees for four blessings was a bargain for the prediction of a blessed future. It would take some time for them to articulate the prophecies, we would do this over lunch at Haveli Restaurant at Jalandhar. It became very obvious to me that many of the Hijras we interacted with had a measure of EQ, emotional intelligence because they possessed a robust emotional vocabulary, meaning that they, more than most people, are able to express what they feel more effectively; and it's true, their contagious positive emotions triggered in us enhancing mood-elevating experiences by just being around them.

Sitting down whilst ordering our food, Sandhya revealed Ajay's past life regression saying he was a prince killed by the Greeks at the Beas River in 326BCE, son of the brave Raja Porus. The sudden revelation of this life regression was immensely pleasing to Ajay who kept silent betrayed only by his facial expressions, raising the eyebrow, opening eyelids and dropped jaw. Over the years he had told me as did Amara his mother that he once was a handsome Indian prince, now it was verified by a stranger, coincidence; who knows?

Meeting the Hijra community was not the only time we met them. They were present big time at the wedding we attended later. One thing was for sure, we had so much in common as far as Human Rights, Social Justice and Equality and the dignity of humankind issues were concerned. They too were not ignorant of western culture; we began to feel we were soul companions.

Sandhya says there are an estimated 6 million Hijras in India, living predominantly in their own communities called Gharana. Many still live on the margins of society but find security and love in their own communities, even though they have a 4000-year-old tradition in Hindu culture, according to the ancient Vedic books. The Hijra community favours Vedic archetypes such as avatar Lord Shiva who presents as half female and male. He/she destroys negativity clearing the way for renewal and growth.

Shamefully, the Christian British were the ones that encouraged ordinary Indians to practice vilification and ostracising and encouraging purges against the Hijra. In 1897 they shamefully criminalized the ancient Hijras. During the British ostracizing period, their royal privileges allowed them to practice a code language now known as Hijra Farsi; that language was forbidden and taken away. They are now, albeit slowly through the courts, regaining their former status in Indian society.

Sandhya says, "Sure we have difficulties, we're outgoing, flirtatious, love to dress up, perform and have our photos taken, yet we meet all these difficulties in our lives with a good sense of humour. However, time is up for the haters and the ignorant. It is always the other people whom we have to consider and accommodate, usually the busybodies, the anxious, the fearful, the unread and unstudied, the superstitious and the easily gullible and unthinking ones. It is rarely the rational people and it gets a bit tiring to always lower oneself to the lowest common denominator of society. Well, I tell them the times are changing; we will speak up, act up and show through our lives that we contribute positively to society. Together with the GLBTIQ community, we bring beauty, brilliance, form and more colour to Indian society. We carve the statues, paint the pictures, take the photos and make films that define humanity, enlightening and elevating all people."

Like many transgender people all over the world, many lead double lives to avoid stigma and discrimination. They wear female clothes and adopt feminine names while mixing in daily life but dress in male clothes if they are male when visiting relatives. Often the feminine role is denied maintaining two distinct lifestyles consequently resulting in an identity crisis of fear, anxiety and depression, so severe that it can lead to suicide. Compulsory fatherhood is a big pressure in India. You have to have babies, you have to be married, and you have to be a father.

Kaif, with a tear of fear in his eyes, says, "There is a housing crisis for the Hijra homeless. We don't want to be children of the pavement anymore." Today, as I finish writing this book, small but big opportunities continue to open up for Hijras. Examples are; India's first transgender lawyer, Sathyasri Sharmila shunning the stereotypical mindset. She became subject to torture because of her gender. Joyita Mondal at the age of 29, India's first transgender judge. First transgender police officer, sub-inspector Prithika Yasini; college principal, Manabi Bandopadhyay – a professor and also becoming the first transgender person in India who completed a Doctor of Philosophy (PhD).

CHAPTER 8

ON THE ROAD TO BEAS

"India has lots of seasonings of affections to wit and here we were ending our journey on the oldest, longest, and one of the magnificent man-made roads in the world, at the junction of the time immemorial Beas River"

I'd be telling you a lie if I said it wasn't hot; the sun was piping hot, shining all the way from New Delhi travelling on the Grand Trunk Road to Beas, 12 hours away. This Grand Trunk Road is not just any old road; it is Asia's oldest and longest, linking the Indian sub-continent with central Asia. It was built by the founder of the first Indian Empire *Chandragupta* in 300BCE beginning at Chittagong, Bangladesh to West Bengal across Northern India to Delhi, passing through Amritsar on towards Lahore and Peshawar in Pakistan, and finally terminating in Kabul, Afghanistan. Little would I realize that this road would frame my memory for a long time to come, not dissimilar to the road of life where everything happens as we travel life's perilous journeys avoiding the potholes and collisions with all the vagaries of our existence.

Darius quickly dubbed it the "GTR" because of the continuous hum and roar of big, colourful transport trucks,

Here on the 2700 km Great Trunk Road, over two thousand years old and the longest road in the world, India's modernity was seen and nothing much was coy nor conservative...the messages on the trucks and advertising boards seen along this ancient road were filled with innuendo and subtleties.

passenger cars, motorcycles, mopeds, horse and carts, bicycles, sounding like an everlasting India on the move roaring into the future, moving towards its never-ending destiny as it has been doing for thousands of years: not just a little road. It is magnificent even today, comparable to the best four-lane freeways anywhere in the world. This 2500-year-old road built by ancient infrastructure engineers of millennials past, maintained and upgraded by modern methods, still works. Thought up by the ancient visionaries, planned and made for the future, still catering to the transportation needs of people, goods and services, fulfilling needs for 1.4 billion Indians. There are no feelings of isolation nor of remoteness when driving on the GTR, not with having hundreds of enthusiastic Indian drivers in cars, and mopeds continually trying to avoid collisions in what looked like never-ending road anarchy. I mean it's not like travelling in the very sparsely populated Australian outback, not one dull moment; the bombardment of all our senses continues 24/7 on this road where you never 'not see' people and a constant buzz of economic activity along its perimeters. There was not a Kilometre to spare where we did not see people going about their business activities or relieving themselves on agricultural land, thousands of road vendors selling refreshments, home-wares, cloth makers, wool spinners, Ayurveda Indian medicine dispensing anti-diarrhoea and headache herbs, clothes, flower and plants nurseries besides the hundreds of petrol stations and their eateries with personal services dotted along the 2700 km long road, one of the longest in the world.

School busses carried frank advertising posters about family planning, picturing condoms and other birth control devices. "Nothing coy or conservative about these," Darius noted, saying, "Let's forever dismiss the myth that India is a conservative society on the basis of the advertising slogans carried on trucks and buses." Students going to Colleges or Universities situated along the GTR enthusiastically waved at us as we paid our tolls at the many toll gates. I began to realize that we were a bit of a novelty due to being the only tall white faces about with blue eyes, Darius's blonde hair and Ajay, while Punjabi, looked much more Southern European than Indian, or maybe it was because of our European designed, not same-same clothes made in China. "We are definitely a point of difference," Darius winked. "Want to see India? Then travel on this road," said Ajay who was proudly telling us about the visual glories of modern India as he drove over the speed limits. As foreigners, the business of driving in India was a gut-wrenching experience; grateful to arrive alive at Beas in the heat of the day.

Surprisingly, at Beas, the temperature was several degrees lower no doubt cooled by the mighty 470 Km long, fast-flowing Beas River, its icy waters originating in Himachal Pradesh far into the Himalayas refreshing the temperature around the small town of Beas. The river has its own *Indus Dolphins* evolved over millions of years. It is also the home of the almost extinct Gharial crocodile. We were overjoyed to hear that a few months before we arrived, 22 Gharial crocodiles were released at Beas, the first phase of reintroducing them to their original home, the Beas River.

Ajay tells us that Project Crocodile was first initiated by the Indian Government in 1975 as a rebreeding project. India has lots of seasonings of affections to wit and here we were ending our journey on the oldest, longest, and one of the most magnificent man-made roads in the world, at the junction of the time immemorial Beas River. It is historically famous for obstructing and stopping Alexander the Great's invasion of India in 326BC when the GTR was already in existence. "Just let that sink in," Darius said. "Yes, and thank God there are no endless legions of tourist groups around this area."

Exiting the great GTR, entering Beas, with a population about 5000, where the past meets the present, where everything was made and designed to human scale, narrow streets not made for cars but perfect for mopeds, a small microcosm of India. Beautiful Beas, the town with no pubs, butchers and grog shops; instead, has one of the best free and public hospitals not to mention the cleanest railway station in India. Streets lined with Frangipani trees, sweet exotic fragrance wafting everywhere.

There was this large iron wrought gate. There were many decorated crafted iron and wooden gates beautifying the small streets and tiny laneways of Beas. We stopped at a three-story large house built of concrete and painted bright pink. Sitting inside beside the gate sat Ajay's 93-year-old grandmother, Nusha who welcomed us with the biggest smile initiating the immediate feel of pleasantness, inclusion, and comfort.

In one of the living rooms on the second floor, we met Amara, Ajay's mum pressing hands together with a smile and a soft Namaste; we mirrored the same. I remembered her as a shy and quiet, but delightful woman from our English class in Melbourne, especially for her elegant saris. The housemaid, Nandini, her name means "bringer of joy" immediately served filtered ice cold water with much-added graciousness and a twinkle in her eyes. Strange, I thought everybody drank in quietness; obviously, the 12-hour trip from Delhi was exhausting.

Darius and Ajay fell sound asleep on the comfortable Diwan couches made for stretching and sleeping, hugging soft fabric cushions, the multitude of embroidered with motifs of the Gods. I was uncomfortable with everybody's quietness. Darshan, sensing my disquiet, smiled and assured me that in India, it perfectly OK to sit in a room where people just sit in quietness and there is no need to talk constantly. He took me up to the apartment within the complex where we were going to stay for a couple of weeks. The upper room was styled like an apartment with kitchenette, shower and toilets and bedroom ceiling cooling fans powered by solar panels. There was a water filter and Darshan warned not to drink tap water and used boiled water to brush my teeth, and there was plenty of toilet paper! The rooms were very welcoming, refurbished and painted in earthy tones, rich browns and burnt bright orange for the walls and the floors were just marble, marble everywhere and opulent looking drapes made from embroidered fabric.

There was a huge balcony around the rooms and on top of the houses for hanging up the washed clothes and for kids to play. Often we would see children flying many colourful kites. Evocative of my own childhood and to actually see kids playing outside in the narrow streets was a wonder. We don't see that in Australia anymore, no kids flying kites like kids do in India. Teenagers spend much time on their electric mopeds.

On Mondays, all the Beas women hang out their multi-coloured washed clothes on their rooftop balconies, showing that India is definitely the land of colour and masters in fabric design. I am comparing that with the shades of washing in Australia where the mass-produced K-mart and target fashion have limited colour range – grey and white and lighter shades in between. The cars in India are also much more colourful than in Australia where most cars are white or grey or shades making roads there dull and boring; but not in India.

There was also a caretaker's and security guard cottage on the roof where Brahmdev, our security guard lives. His name means "God's exalted angel". Darshan tells me he is a *Jat Punjabi*. We had met *Jat Punjabi* men in Melbourne; they are usually taxi drivers, very honest, funny and energetic. "I have to admit," says Darius, "they try to be overtly masculine always feeling they have to prove themselves; slightly insecure, masculine in the traditional sense of the word they're passionate about showing off big cars, smart phones, loud music, and they are vegetarians. They can't live without milk, curd, ghee and they love their buffaloes. Most of the Jat men are agricultural workers, not much given to study other than agriculture."

After taking a very cold water shower and refreshing our clothes, Darius and I were resting on a large King-size bed, not soft but very firm by western standards.

Brahmdev walks in, introduces himself and just sits on the bed. We got used to people just walking in and sitting on our large beds, to chat and share a meal. Did we say something about community and collectivism? Brahmdev runs a sports centre and trampoline business proudly showing off pictures of his family and his much-loved imported, spotlessly, shiny-black chrome *Harley Davidson* motorcycle, a very important status symbol. Eventually, like every Indian we encountered, he asks, "How do you like India?" We quickly discovered that to just say 'we like it' superficial of the cuff cliché is considered rude. So there and then I decided to write a book with the help of Darius and Ajay about my perceptions of India and its people and why I loved and liked it.

Nusha, the mother of Amara lived in one of the self-contained rooms on the ground floor next to the large Iron entry gate along the narrow busy street where she keeps track of the comings and goings of friends, neighbours and familiar faces, she had known for decades. Her small window facing the street doubles like a sweet and wisdom dispenser where young children sing to her and she dispenses sweets. Younger teenagers see her like an aunty and they come and ask her for advice or just to show her their new mopeds or Apples, Galaxies; she knows everything, in a nice way that is.

Older people in India are indeed the mortar that holds nearly all of the Indian life together. Neighbours just come and chat and share some of their delicious vegetarian food. What a difference between India and the west where Ageism is practised to the utmost. Here in India, older people are venerated for their wisdom and as Darius cheekily says, "In Australia, they are venerated for their dollar." These neighbourhood conversations, music, children playing and singing in Beas's small streets are guaranteed to banish old age isolation as there is in the west. I had noticed that Indian families do not get rid of their elderly in old age homes as they do in the west. No, here the elderly are treasured, venerated and respected for their wisdom and cared for. Old age is not an affliction but a great blessing. There is no discrimination against old people. We, in the west, are not smart when it comes to old age and in Australia, the pensioners are the poorest; what a different story in India.

CHAPTER 9

BEAS BARBER SHOP CONVERSATIONS

Indian people always seemed intrigued why we're so fascinated by their country. They wanted to know the whys and wherefores and what we liked best about them. It is not something one can answer in glib common throwaway cliches that would be disrespectful Darius said. They themselves felt that they were not as materially well off as westerners and often made excuses for their lack of sophistication when they compared themselves with us. We tried to explain that sophistication is only relevant to the culture one lives in. Often, when we were invited into their humble homes for a meal, they would scramble to find a fork, knife and spoon for us to eat despite the fact we were perfectly at ease eating with our fingers.

We perceived that Indians are much more content and happier than most westerners, frequently quoting our favourite cliché, "you never see yourself as others see you" but, what did we think of the five disabled beggars sitting on the Beas railway overpass? "That's nothing, wait until you see the thousands of homeless people and beggars in Australia sleeping raw in the streets in our major and provincial cities." The surprised looks of their disbelief are forever etched in my memory. They could not understand that this happens in Australia too because their children's friends who study in Australia never mention the poverty and

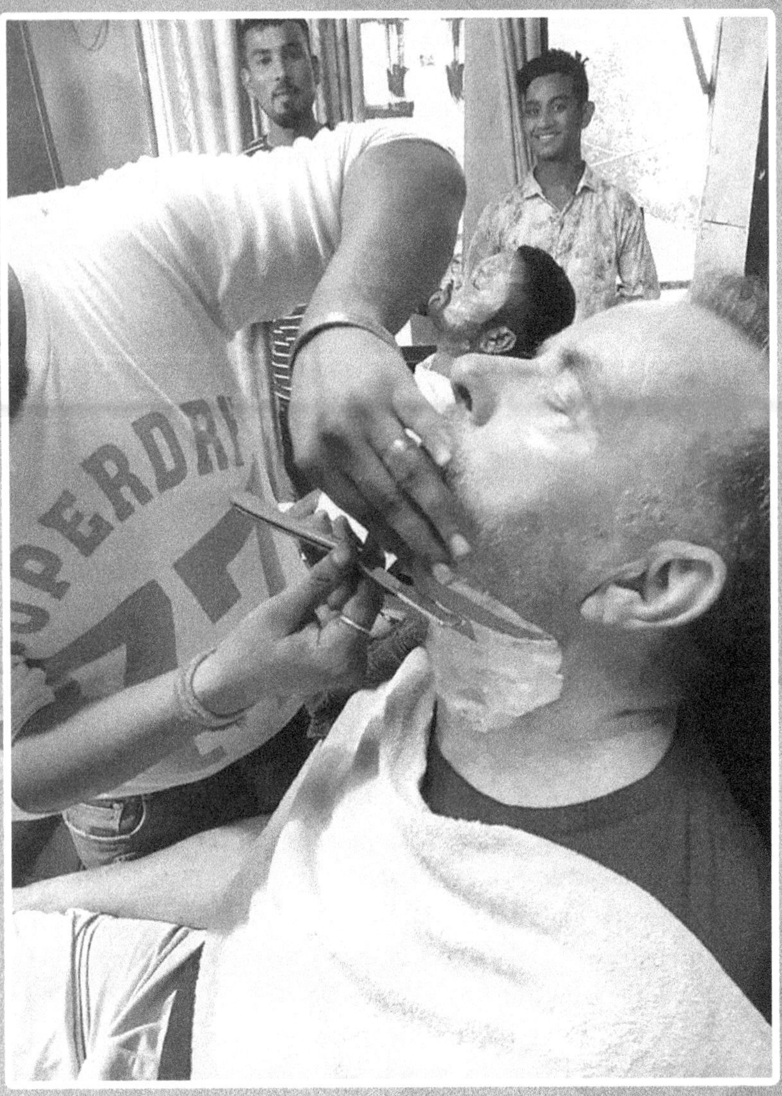

I had my beard trimmed. In fact, not just a trim, three young men apprenticed hairdressers and male beauty consultants would exfoliate the skin, clean and massage your face and neck followed by a good shaving lather, ready to be shaved by an old-fashioned cut-throat blade. My blade was 76 years old and had shaved many faces including the face of the very famous one, Mahatma Gandhi, who had been shaved by the same blade I was shaved with; I had no reason to doubt. Everything and anything in India is related to the past morphed into the present. Their whole philosophy and way of life seem like this.

social dysfunction of Australian society with their suicides sky-high, domestic violence and alcoholism and the overwhelming dysfunctional problems due to drugs not seen in India on a scale such as in Australia. It is more in your face there than here in Beas. It was better here as we could see you carry the disabled beggars to their overnight shelters for feeding and showering.

In my country, I am ashamed to say the homeless sleep rough underneath the awnings of shops in the Central Business districts of our large cities. I like India because its society is much more connected with each other, people actually care more, old people are venerated; there is value for life, animals have the same rights because they are sentient, people are more into the community than anywhere else in the world.

Secondly, I like India because its people are much more connected with each other and their economic activity is not as manipulative and corrupt as western neo-liberal capitalism. Economic customs here in India are over 4000 years old, showing that communal traditions and religion are the regulators of their collective minded society. This was quite evident in the hundreds of businesses, street bazaars and small processing and manufacturing units even in a small place such as Beas. India is not a secular state as we know secular in the west, yet their style of government and business was protean and continues to adjust to the modern world without sacrificing their ancient culture.

Amara called out that our food was being served. Nandini had prepared our dinner under her guidance. I knew that many of the vegetarian cookeries were very different from my vegetarian cooking. Actually, I was vegan, but that was very hard to be in India. I did not use dairy products primarily because of the cruelty done to cows. For a cow to give milk, the mother cow has to be lactating all the time and this means giving birth to a calf. In Australia, the calf gets taken away from the mother so it can't drink the milk and calves are killed or bred in small boxes where they become anaemic so their veal stays white. "Oh, the cruelty of it all," Darius grumbled. In India, cows are royalty as are their calves and are not usually bred for veal. Having justified to myself that the milk was produced without cruelty to mother cow, we decided to just eat vegetarian, drink milk and use ghee and drink lassi.

Fun Conversation at the Beas Barber Shop.

Once every three days, we'd go to the hairdressers to have our beards trimmed. Darius, on the other hand, went for a clean shave and some waxing to have some hair on his back and chest removed; it would show up his muscles, he said and made him feel more desirable. "Everyone wants to feel desirable," the apprentice beauty consultant said, adding that making people feel good and desirable about themselves is their livelihood. Without that good feeling, they would not have a job.

Of course, at the Barber's shop, we would meet many Indian men with whom we could have a serious, funny and enlightening conversation about anything. The Punjabi men are very proud of their masculinity and are concerned with the presentation of self in their everyday life. They dress really well, having a peculiar Indian look such as wearing a turban contrasted by a cool western look as shown by the barbershop boys who wore low-waist jeans that exposed their underwear brand on the elastic band. Darius said, "They want to expose their masculinity and show off their expensive underwear brand to impress the girls or others." The poor and the rich wear jewellery to enhance their masculinity as women their femininity. So, I had my beard trimmed. In fact, not just a trim, three young men apprenticed hairdressers and male beauty consultants would exfoliate the skin, clean and massage your face and neck followed by a good shaving lather, ready to be shaved by an old-fashioned cut-throat blade. My blade was 76 years old and had shaved many faces including the face of the very famous one, Mahatma Gandhi, who had been shaved by the same blade I was shaved with; I had no reason to doubt. Everything and anything in India is related to the past, morphed into the present. Their whole philosophy and way of life seem like this.

India is a culture of science mixed with an equal portion of spirituality invented by great sages who were also great scientists. The Punjabi men reminded us, westerners, that an Indian scholar named Aryabhata wrote, in 5AD, that the earth and other astral bodies were spherical and that the earth rotates around the sun. That was almost 1000 years before Nicolaus Copernicus put forth the theory (1543) that the Sun is at rest near the centre of the universe, and that the Earth, spinning on its axis once daily, revolves annually around the Sun, calling it the heliocentric, or Sun-centred system. Another Indian scientist and sage, Saint Bhaskaracharya discovered the law of gravity 1200 years before Isaac Newton. He also calculated that the time required to rotate around the sun is 365.258756484 days and the latest western scientific calculation is 365.2596 days. Not much of an error for a calculation made 1200 years ago. We knew that was true yet the western education system all but ignores the contribution of the Indian or Asian scientists. We were astounded at all this knowledge and learning being exposed and amazed at the Beas barbershop where we met extraordinary people.

Beas was like a small microcosm of India. Everything was made locally, everyone had a job either working for themselves or others. One would just not sit around doing nothing; there were no unemployment benefits. Amara had sent me to the dairy early in the morning, when it was still cool, with a two-litre stainless steel canister. At the dairy, Aunty Noona, the dairy-woman used her two-litre ladle to fill the canister with unpasteurised milk. Amara would boil the milk always before serving. I took with me another smaller canister for sour Lassi and Yoghurt. The recipe for these two dairy products was thousands of years old and made from a Greek recipe brought to Punjab by Alexander the Great's descendants who settled in and around Beas.

After the Dairy visit, Darius carried a heavy bag of wheat, 100 kilos, to the miller for flour. Once it was ground, it was split into 50 kg bags so we carried one each, but imagine a miller! We don't have those in the west anymore. Then, there was the cobbler mending shoes and the tailor sewing suits, the bakeries for fresh bread and sweets and it was all very modern. What impressed me was that very little was mass-produced. There was absolutely nothing made in China, even the thousands of electronic mopeds so very popular with the teenagers were made in India and assembled locally in Beas, creating employment for local people who all seemed to walk to work. There was a movie studio where they made local movies such as Indian weddings. The fruit and vegetable stores were in abundance with almost every known fruit available. Vegetables were locally grown and fresh. There was no supermarket in Beas, instead, it had a vibrant patchwork of street bazaars ideal for daily chit chat, or friendly affirmative gossip.

Beas was not a typical Indian village. It had no grog or butcher shops and smoking was not encouraged, yet there was always a happy atmosphere in the hustle and bustle in the seven streets, which all looked like Bazaars where one could socialize with local people and sip Chai Latte or drink coffee in the many cafes and tea houses. Ajay explains to us that chai in Hindi is just tea. The British introduced tea from China to India as well as milk and sugar. They fed this to the Indian slaves who worked at the plantation. Drinking Chai was one of their payments. Masala chai is quite special with grated ginger, black pepper, cardamom and cinnamon sticks. The slurping sound they make while drinking tea indicates enjoyment.

CHAPTER 10

DERA, A VISION OF FUTURE INDIA

Darshan and Amara invited us to join them at the Beas community centre in meditation and breakfast very early in the morning. There was no need to set our alarm clocks for four am; the Hindu Temple choruses started chanting at three-thirty am sounding almost like haunting yet beautiful Gregorian chants, mysterious, intriguing and energetic. Darius and I did not want to turn over and go back to sleep; the chanting would surely keep us awake. Both taking a quick brisk cold shower putting on our white T-shirt and woollen jumpers; we figured white is purity, long pants a must, we were specially told not to wear shorts as we do in Australia, men's legs are apparently erotic. Darshan served a quick cup of tea warming up our innards after the cold showers fortifying us against the very cold morning temperatures of three degrees.

Outside the house, a three-wheeled tuk-tuk, a type of motor rickshaw, was waiting to take us to the Dera town, the large gated place of meditation. A meeting place of peaceful humanity established in 1889 by the Radha Soami, a philosophical movement that encompasses all peaceful humanitarian religious and philosophical views. They live in word and deed promoting non-violence, meditation, vegetarianism and treating the body as a clean, living Temple; that was a great attraction for us.

Our young, new-found friends were also going to the Beas's Radha Soami Hospital as medical interns offering sewa. The Radha Soami collective has four other charitable hospitals all in rural India, including many scattered 24/7 clinics. Everyone is helped inclusive of caste status wealthy or poor, including physiotherapy and dental care. This just wasn't any standard charitable hospital, staffed by best medical Doctors and specialists from all over India who come for a season working without pay to do their Sewa service; these are cardiologists, oncologist, urologists and ophthalmologist.

Experiencing, seeing, feeling and meeting people who practised these kinds of philosophical lifestyles was what we were looking for. Picking the fruits of their ancient wisdom, what could we learn, how could we be enriched by knowledge, how could our trust in humanity be restored, we were full of anticipation and quiet excitement.

The tuk-tuk only had room for six people, four large women had already taken their seats wearing much gold jewellery, pierced noses and tikas on their foreheads. We too had a Tika on our forehead placed there by Tey, our young Brahmin Hindu Priest (who had come down from New Delhi) before boarding the tuk-tuk. It became a squeeze noticing the delight in the faces of the Indian women when Darius and I, tall well-built whitefaces gingerly took our places beside them, real close. Sitting so close that my nose almost rubbed her nose. She smiled showing rows of gold plated teeth, and a stud on her pierced tongue, thankful that everyone was hygienic and spotlessly clean wearing fresh clothes, a blessing in a culture with little awareness of personal space. The drive to the Dera took 15 minutes, to the bus and tuk-tuk terminals. Hundreds of buses were unloading their human cargos in almost reverential silence. On arrival, everyone had to hand in their mobile phones before we could enter what looked like a gated community. Thousands of people were streaming like water through the security gates; bodies and bags being scanned, just like airport security.

Darshan had explained that the whole Radha Soami organization is run by thousands of volunteers called Sewadars (volunteers offering service for free) who offer their services as Sewa (meaning selfless service) relentlessly driven by spiritual energy and love and a devotion to service humanity.

We arrived about two hours before the actual commencement of the Satsang, necessary to take our place early. The logistics of seating all the expected three hundred and fifty thousand people decently and in order takes time. The Satsangis (students) came today to hear the Master teacher *Gurinder Singh Dhillon.* Krishna, in the meantime, had joined us with some of his friends introducing us charmingly while we were sipping tea. Darius noted the contrast of meeting people at a bar and meeting people via the ritual of sipping tea at the Dera. The effect is the same, meeting people. "Life is all about people," Krishna says, whereupon I spontaneously sing Barbra Streisand's song "People who need people are the luckiest people." Other friendly Indians, yet ever so inquisitive, join in with our spontaneity. Any stereotypical ideas about Indians being kind of shy and conservative was not bearing out, here at the Dera, there is total inclusion; any shyness or pretentions before going to the main Satsang evaporates.

We were awed by the size of the auditorium, although to us it looked more like a highly sophisticated sheep holding shed; only this one was huge, built to fit five hundred thousand people! It has the world's largest iron roof with 21 acres of solar panels and a dust-free clay and cow dung floor to reduce any echoing. By 9.30 am, thirty-five thousand are sitting cross-legged on the floor, women separated from the men, male children with their fathers, female children with their mothers. Darius and Krishna sit with the men crossed-legged for three hours on the floor. I being a westerner am offered a chair in a special section for Europeans and others including the very elderly and disabled, who can't sit cross-legged for hours on the floor. Foreigners are provided with translating earphones for translation into English.

During the seating of the hundreds of thousands of people, not a sound is heard except the gentle sound of the sacred Vedic hymns including Tina Turner singing her children's Peace Mantra *Sarvesham Svastir Bhavatu* and the gentle swishing of hundreds of ceiling fans and evaporative coolers. We are intrigued how all these people are going to be fed, I wonder if Jesus will lose his claim of miraculously feeding the 5000 with bread that would now be a nothing event when compared. Were we about to bear witness to a much more miraculous event of how three hundred and fifty thousand people are going to be fed all at once, a three-course meal served all in one on stainless steel plates with indented spaces for three varieties of food – one vegetable, bread roti and yoghurt with sour lassi.

"Nothing is miraculous," Darshan says everything is logistically and meticulously planned, not one thing is left to chance or good luck. After seeing the production lines in the *Langar* (kitchen), we are convinced planning is the key and not miracles. Two million Chai lattes in 30 minutes are served, how is this even possible? The large tea-making Langar where 1500 *Sewadars*, a mix of male and female, work and sing harmonious Vedic hymns while making and serving tea made by 30 huge automated tea vessels each producing 1120 litres of tea every hour. The tea is pumped through pipes to the serving areas where trained tea *sewadars* pour eighty thousand litres of tea per hour. It is not just ordinary tea, it is made with all the real herbs, easy to experience a "magic mushroom moment". We said this because having tried magic mushrooms in Nederland, we knew the effect was the same.

Imagine having 1000 professional *sewadars* who are rolling one million Rotis or Chapatis per mealtime; each chapati is coated by Ghee, clarified butter that originated in ancient India. Rotis, Chapatis, Naan, Paneer, Dal and Dosa are made from locally grown stone-ground wholemeal flour and wheat is stored in several huge 2000 ton silos. *Sewadars* harvest, glean and sieve the flour.

It is not only the Rotis that are served on our stainless steel plates but also generous portions of totally vegan *Korma* loaded with potatoes, tomatoes, carrots and peas, naan Indian bread and several types of delicious dips. There are no eating utensils required, Indian people use their fingers, and only whitefaces such as us are given stainless steel forks and spoons out of respect for our ways of having food. A million native Indian mangos freshly picked from Dera's own very large mango growing orchards are cut and mixed with milk products provided by their freely roaming holy cows. Darius and I considered Mango as holy nectar given by the Vedic love Gods, a nutritionally complete drink providing all of the 21 amino acids essential for life.

I am not sure if the novelty of us was the reason why so many people invited us to join their families to eat and socialize with them. Thousands of family and friends groups were spread out sitting around on the grass underneath the myriads of large trees, fragranced and coloured by flower hedges and exotic scrubs in wide parklands shaded from the hot sun. The size and enormous amounts of everything including social customs was a constant reminder that we were in an ancient nation of 1.3 billion people, and there were few comparisons with a small thinly populated Continent nation like Australia.

There are three notable things that stood out; older people are revered and cared for and fed by the younger generation; not one plastic bottle in sight, nothing plastic not even wrappers, there are no wrappers because everything is freshly made; 20 first-aid stations with dispensaries during the Satsang program. Darius is anxious to pay for our tea, eager not to be freeloaders; westerns do have a 'freeloader' reputation in India, gained when the hippies of the 1960s came to India to meditate, seek enlightenment, loaf and space out. Darshan prepared and gave us the special vouchers for tea, and main meals and Lassies, however, those who did not have vouchers were also fed.

Sustainable infrastructures are seen everywhere – roads, buildings, utilities are all around Dera. Even walking on the wide and clean perfectly designed footpaths themselves is work of art, not just any old footpaths or road. There are 4000 brick men and women *sewadars* working periodically on these roads, not all at once. They're wearing safety glasses while smashing damaged bricks with hammers powered by muscle and elbow crease, using the smashed pieces as foundation road fillers. The bricks come from the local community's ultra-modern, environmentally sound bricks making Kiln that produced fifty thousand bricks every day, not to mention the thousands of ceramic tiles made at the tiles' workshops. All tars bitumen is produced in-house, road tarring employs 1000 *sewadar* volunteers and takes place in June – July, the hottest months during the hottest part of the day in sweltering heat because the tar has to be pliable to be poured over the foundation road bricks. Construction work is constantly going on; a state of the art mini airport is also being built at Dera.

The buildings are all very modern in what looks like Art Deco architecture. For all the buildings including the hospitals, schools, shopping centre, timeless design is made from locally produced sustainable materials at Dera's carpentry paint and iron workshops.

Cleaning: An Army of 1000 disciplined and enthusiastic *sewadars* get up at three am every morning before the influx, at times up to a million people come during Satsangs, they are assigned to clean and sanitize the streets, washrooms and roads. The *sewadars* believe they are the fortunate ones and that Dera is a gift from God so who does not want to keep it clean as well as cleansing their own mind through meditation.

A big recycling plant ensures everything and anything is recycled; nothing goes to waste. Bio-oxidation ponds provide recycled drink and grey-water for irrigation, non-biodegradable materials are sold or sent for recycling, empty milk cartons are used for growing seedling. Indians take climate change seriously. We spent several days helping to plant trees. The proof of this sustainable recycling was given by a NASA out in space photograph showing India and China to be the only places on earth to increase their forest and green places. Australia showed deforestation and a barren place by comparison.

Agricultural production: So, where does all the food come from? The Dera has 1900 acres of farmlands, fruit orchards, market gardens and diary. It is the most self-sustainable complex in India. These Dera farms provide nearly all the food. 60 percent of the land is dedicated to green areas and all produce grown on 1100 acres is organic. Rainwater is harvested self-sustainable in agricultural produce.

Krishna showed us the 500-seat modern library at Dera that constantly endeavours to acquire and requisition many books on Sant Mat, (teaching of all the saints and philosophers) books that would explain the Science of the Soul. This library reminded me of the 700-year Alexandria library accidentally burnt down after the siege of Alexandria in 48BCE whose motto was similar to the Library at Dera "the place for a cure of the soul" with thousands of books on mysticism and philosophy and science. Then, there was this ancient book restoration department repairing, preserving and restoring old text. The wisdom of the ages preserved and restored.

We are asked if we want to donate blood before going to have a look at the Beas Dera Hospital. The thousands of people attending the Dera were all donating blood, just as well we have our Red Cross blood donation cards with us. Blood donations are taken by nurses dressed in the most colourful saris, their Tikas and Nath in place; friendly, quick and efficient. Blood donation puts emphasis on our common humanity and makes us realize that all human blood is the same regardless of race and culture; we all share a common ancestry, how true that is. Other free blood tests are also included for sugar diabetes, prostate, and breast cancer or any sexually transmitted diseases.

Our tuk-tuk, on the way back to Beas, is cramped in with six energetic young men all seeming to be *Pehelwani* wrestlers. Surprised that our young, new-found friends were also going to the Beas's Radha *Soami Hospital* as medical interns offering sewa. *The Radha Soami collective* has four other charitable hospitals all in rural India, including many scattered 24/7 clinics. Everyone is helped inclusive of caste status wealthy or poor, including physiotherapy and dental care. This just wasn't any standard charitable hospital, staffed by best medical Doctors and specialists from all over India who come for a season working without pay to do their *Sewa* service; these are cardiologists, oncologist, urologists and ophthalmologist.

On the day we were the guest at the Dera and Beas hospital, 300 cataract operations had been done in the ophthalmologist section of the hospital at no cost to the patient. Darshan asked me how much I paid in Australia for my cataract operation. "Oh, only a mere three thousand dollars per eye," but then, nothing much in the west is for the collective good as is the case in India.

This hospital also does stem cell transplants and research, organ harvesting and transplanting, including Brain surgeries are performed daily, often beyond the basics of medical procedures. On the day we were there, 46 kidneys, 30 human lungs and hearts, plus 26 eyes were harvested. No one got paid and recipients receive organs free. Indians have such enlightening ideas about these things, but Aussies are very iffy about organ harvest euthanasia and these sort of things that have been a part of the Vedic culture for thousands of years.

Preventative medicine is practised at every stage; people are educated on how to prevent disease aided by the *Sattvic* and *Ayurveda* lifestyles promoting healthy nutrition, not one size fits the lot but based upon individual needs. Electrocardiogram (EGC), hearing and vision tests are given to all attendees free of charge with a guaranteed test result given overnight. In the west, it appears that "a patient healed is a dollar lost". This is especially the case in the USA but the reverse is true in India "a stitch in time save nine". One million patients are treated annually at these hospitals either with western medicine alternative homeopathy or *Ayurveda*. There was also sizable dental care available.

Darius, who amongst nutrition had also studied architecture, was impressed with the eco-architectural and aesthetically pleasing buildings at Dera and particularly the Beas Dera Hospital built in the style of Art Deco pleasing to the eye. In the west, the price of a building goes up when it is environmentally friendly; in India, it is the opposite, the price goes down. Elsewhere in India, these country hospitals are 100% energy efficient with natural light and fresh air, lawns and gardens designed for patients to heal outside on manicured shaded lawns. Medical Campus with excellent infrastructure, housing staff and facilities.

It became so much apparent to me that in India, both in the countryside and in the cities, there is generally so much more collective care for community and fellow humans, as compared with the individualism in the west where the "me-me" smartphone generation is generally selfish, especially if they are devoid of a social conscience. Patients come here empty-handed, there is no financial motive for the doctors and nurses but their altruistic service to help make these mostly poor people remain healthy enough to go back to work because their families depend on them to work.

There are hundreds of Dera and Ashram types of communities that serve millions of people. They are the mortar that holds this society together, not unlike social security that western governments have. These thousands of sewadars serve with the spirit of love and compassion rarely seen on planet earth.

CHAPTER 11

A HINDU WEDDING

Ajay created a lot of excitement when he invited Darius and me to Jag and Misha's wedding even though we had already planned to experience India. The wedding invitation gave us extra impetus to actually book a plane ticket. The invitation further piqued my curiosity of a big brash colourful Hindu wedding, the ones you see in Bollywood movies full of attractive looking energetic Indians going wild dancing.

Jag had fallen in love with Misha when he interviewed her for a job. She got the job because it was love at first sight; their marriage was not arranged only through serendipity. They were an individualistic couple, independent non-conformist up to a point, having western tastes and aspirations. Yet tradition took precedence over western modernity, the lifestyle of choice by Indian millennials living in the large cities. Every single custom and practice in a Hindu wedding ceremony has deep philosophical and spiritual significance. Being unique amongst other traditions throughout the world, Hindus adhere to thousands of years of traditional sets of rituals. As a contrast, in the west, people can get married without any ceremony, just two people and one witness, and a hollowed one-lined clichéd of "enduring love and loyalty" plus a fee for the registrar and you are done in five minutes.

Bride promises to the Groom saying "Lalayami cha pade vadet" I will decorate myself with jewellery, with garlands of flowers, ensuring euphoria of my fragrance just for you and serve you in every way possible, and I will promise not to nag you.

The preparation for this wedding was phenomenal; there is so much precedence, cultural aspects to consider. The design of the wedding invitations had to be attractive with some cultural yet contemporary imaginary because many of the guests were the young millennial generation, colleagues from Jag's IT Company where he was the manager. Then there was the secrecy surrounding the marriage announcements, facing a dilemma due to the fact that Misha, his forthcoming bride, also worked for the same company whose policy forbade relatives working together. Everything was therefore kept hush-hush until the management of the company gave permission.

Traditional wedding invitations for the villagers of Beas were delivered personally by hand, door to door, by Ajay and his mum Amara. We helped carry the hundreds of red and gold tread satchels filled with thirty or so almonds given to further entice the invitees to accept the invitation. Almonds symbolize health, wealth, happiness, fertility and long life, and in India, they are tokens of good fortune and happiness.

A fast rewind for a moment, on our second day in India, while we were staying at Jag's place in Cybercity, New Delhi, we were taken to choose our two sets wedding costumes, one for the big party with the villagers, and another outfit for the wedding ceremony. The tailors were Muslim; they greeted us with *As-Salamu Alaykum* meaning "Peace be unto you" and we greeted back with *Namaste* meaning "I bow to you". It dawned on me how ordinary Indian people don't really care what kind of religion one has or practice; to wit that, '*here are Muslim tailors making the wedding outfits for a Hindu wedding, fantastic!*' I thought. Tea was served by young boys while measurements were taken and choices of style and materials made. The discussions with tailors, the one elder and the other three younger men, probably apprentices gave much attention to detail and finesse. It struck me that the average Indian is not as empty as the average westerner; they are much more grounded in the spiritual and physical worlds, we were the customers yet it was as though we had known the tailors forever. Our conversations had substance, their down to earthiness touched me. Darius smiled, he knew my dislike for the affected, the namby-pamby, and the pretentious and false class system that the British had left behind in India.

We chose traditional Indian styles, a *Sherwani* jacket and silk-made Dhoti, one outfit for the party was made out of silk with tulip designs on it, especially for me because I was born in The Netherlands and they thought that would be appropriate. The designs were traditional Indian for the actual wedding ceremony. We chose two black patterned, fine wool material body-hugging Indian Nehru Jackets.

The wedding party had a convivial carnival-like atmosphere, stimulating our senses through the aroma of foods and non-alcoholic drinks, tea and freshly brewed coffees. For us whitefaces, coming from Melbourne, the coffee capital of Australia, the fragrance of freshly ground coffee immediately spread like the incense of the realm of the living. On display was the gorgeous glamour of Indian imagery, everything glittered on the swirling multi-coloured saris, real gold, sapphires, pearls and diamonds; here nothing was fake or pretentious. Mingling with guests, introducing ourselves, exchanging flatteries gave us the exhilarating feeling of total acceptance and inclusion. Happily smiling, socializing, singing, gathering around the plethora of Café type pop up bars, Coffee and Tea houses, large vegetarian smorgasbord spreads of delicacies, the likes of which I had never seen before, an Indian sweet shop looking more like a Vienna Chocolate cake shop, gave it a very cosmopolitan global feel. In the relaxed wedding atmosphere, people opened up several asking where my wife was, why I did not bring her with me to India, and what my relationship with Darius was. It was all good-natured so I did not mind answering these personal questions, saying I was still waiting for Babaji (God) to give me a wife; that seemed to satisfy them because they all understood that Babaji has everybody's welfare and life at heart. Honestly, I mirrored the conversation of the people, and a wedding was really no place to go into deep and meaningful discussions.

The presentation of the wedding gifts inside the reception centre was another spectacle of money proportions. Family and some guests were asked to stand on the stage with the bridal couple taking the centre stage, their relatives presented gifts of beautifully crafted paper flowers made from denominations of paper money shown in full view of all the guests. A large flower with red colour solicited a big "ah" from the audience. If it was worth a lot, I could not quite comprehend why one would show off the value of the gifts, but it is a cultural thing and doesn't mean that a cheaper gift is less valued than a more expensive gift. I noticed that the aunties quickly calculated the value of the money flower. Watching the aunties' expression gave an indication of approval or disapproval followed by some friendly, clever and funny gossip. I clapped when they clapped, sang when they sang, and fronted up when they did. Much Punjabi was spoken so my mind was on auto-pilot, and it is best to be that way when one does not fully understand tradition and wedding culture.

Nine am, early on Sunday morning, on the second day of the wedding celebrations we were woken up by a mixture of sounds consisting of bangles, drums, saxophone and joyful singing in the distant streets. Then, suddenly, there was loud knocking reinforced by banging on the large Iron Gate next to our bedroom. Waking up in a hurry, we quickly dressed, got up and walked out to see what all the noise was about. The caretaker had already opened the gates leading into the house. Then, all went quiet morphing into a stream of ethereal looking people gracefully dancing their way accompanied by a euphony of singing, tambourines, flutes and saxophones playing and the clanging of bangles here, there and everywhere. The Hijra community fronted up in full force in beautiful saris draped over their very attractive female bodies "surely intimidating the corpulent homely looking straight women," Darius observed.

After the Hijras' ritual performances and breakfast, we moved to our favourite barber and beauty shop for haircuts, body massages and facials. The oils used refreshed and titillated our moods and bodies looking our best for the wedding feast and ceremony. Back at the house, a beautiful white stallion was waiting for the groom dressed like an Indian prince with all the Hindu accoutrements and jewellery. Indeed it was a royal steed saddled by Jag who rode it like royalty on to the temple for a blessing. Everyone, family, friends and all the Beas villagers followed on foot dancing in a procession known as the *baraat*.

The actual ceremony took place at the Hyatt Hotel garden roof in Amritsar where the Hotel had a *mandap* canopy where the couple with the guests joins hands and circles around a small enclosed fire, the *anga* in a ritual called the *mangal phera*. Now Jag and his bride were ready to take the seven steps of the *saptapadi* where they made vows to love and affirm each other and live happily ever after. If patience is a virtue, I qualify for being virtuous; the ceremony took six hours, that was the longest I had ever sat through, nota bene cross-legged, but I managed with a bit of help from Tey, one of the priests who shared some of his Soma sacred energy drink, wink, it definitely was not boring, it was in fact high fun drama. Darshan had asked Darius to carry a black leather bag; it was heavy and contained a lot of cash. I had tried to lift it and it would have weighed 15 kilos worth of paper money; that's capital. Halfway during the ceremony, the priest stopped, turning to Darshan requesting more money saying he refused to complete the ceremony if more money was not paid. Even though the price had been agreed before, the priest had changed his mind reasoning that "if you can afford to have a wedding at the Hyatt, you can afford to pay more." Haggling pursued for a few minutes and Darius passed on the black heavy leather bag. It was opened and another fifty thousand rupees were handed to the priest, what a drama, but smiling relatives indicated that it was all part of a Hindu ceremony.

The ceremony itself was amazing in its honesty and authenticity. It had a number of points, *Pheras* the Hindus call them, they are about 3000 years old and not changed. The couple prayed to God for blessings then the priest prayed in Sanskrit *"Om esha ekapadi bhava iti prathaman"* a promise which says that each day their love for each other will be more intense than the day before. Jag then had to ask his bride to cook for him and in return, Misha will bestow all her love on him. The Bride says she will wholeheartedly accept the groom's judgment. Then there is a second Phera pleading with God to impart them with mental stability, physical health and spiritual strength so that they can live life without too many hassles and promising to stand by each other forever, "and that's a long time" Darius quipped into my ear.

The Bride pledged as she uttered Kutumburn *rakshayishyammi sa aravindharam,* meaning I will always protect you and our family and children from evil, and I only have 'yes' for you. In other words, she promises not to nag her husband, ever.

In the third Phera, the groom speaks the words *"Om rayas Santu joradastayaha"* we will spiritually abide with each other and I will look at other women only as my sisters. We shall flourish together under God. To this, the bride replies, and I will love other men only as my brothers and my love and devotion for you will never fade. It also included a promise to love and look after the parents in their declining years.

The fourth Phera, the bride and groom commit themselves by saying *"Om mayo bhavyas jaradastaya ha"* to respect and care for our elders and parents. You will bring fortune and sanctity into my life; may God bless us with an ecstatic life and healthy children. The Bride promises to the Groom saying "*Lalayami cha pade vadet*" I will decorate myself with jewellery, with garlands of flowers, ensuring euphoria of my fragrance just for you and serve you in every way possible, and I will promise not to nag you.

During the ceremony, there were several anointing of sweet oil, a form of Holy Spirit inducement that reminded me of the many parallels between Christian, Jewish and Muslim weddings. Darius and I came to the conclusion that a wedding is a wedding; love is love between two special people who promise to stick with each other through thick and thin.

CHAPTER 12

THE AUNTIES, MAYLA, BEDINA AND MAME ARE WALKING MATRIMONY SITES

Aunties, we learnt are the sunshine in all Indian families. When Indians use the term aunty, it might be a term of respect for people older than themselves. Many times the aunties are not blood relations, which to us was quite confusing.

In the past, an Indian village had real aunts and uncles raising nephews and nieces. In the modern age, when Indians are becoming more mobile and nuclear families being the norm, it still takes a village to raise an Indian child but now friends of parents become surrogate uncles and aunts. Darshan explained how to recognize distinctions *Ammayi, Cheriamma* or *Edathi* are used for close family members, these Indian terms lets one know in which pecking order in the family they are. Other Indian names for aunty are *Maami* and *Mausi, and for uncle are Maama and Mausa.*

Hence, on the first day of Jag and Misha's wedding, we met so many of their families and friends. Almost everyone introduced themselves as an aunty or uncle; raising a smile and our eyebrows. Darius commented that many aunties looked and acted almost like *drag queens* reminding and comparing them with Australian drag Queen *Dame Edna Everage,* a much loved and national icon who dresses in women's clothing and acts

I had met Aunty Mayla before the wedding when we delivered the wedding invitation. She lived in a splendid three-story Indian house with roof space for living. The most striking part of her house was the swirling white and beige genuine marble floor. Her real pride and joy was the orange tree, growing many sweet oranges, squeezing fresh orange juice, "only for Australian guests," she smiled with her very white teeth.

with exaggerated feminine gender roles. Like the Indian aunties, Dame Edna Everage was always concerned about marriage, fashion and comparing themselves with the socially upward middle class; a funny but not innocent gossiping sorority, not unlike Hyacinth Bouquet from the British sitcom *Keeping up Appearances* occupied with keeping up appearances, status and class, something we thought the Indians had inherited from the British.

Prior to the wedding, Darshan had taken us with him to deliver the hundreds of invitations by hand, door to door in Beas and in the neighbouring villages. That is how we got to meet several of Ajay's real blood-relative aunties. On the second day of the wedding, we met more new aunties at the Hyatt Hotel in Amritsar; while the young Punjabi guests and Darius were dancing their feet off, I escaped the vigorous dancing because my eardrums were getting an unbearable bashing of earthquake proportions, withdrawing to the outside garden where a large buffet of an international vegetarian cuisine was served. Out of the corner of my eye, pretending to see nothing, I detected several older aunties ordering their husbands around to fill up plates with food and these aunties would then transfer the wedding food into an ice cream container covering the container with large stylish embroidered Indian serviettes that did not look cheap and large enough to cover the plastic container. Inwardly, I smiled, thinking it's no different than us westerners asking for a doggy bag at restaurants if we cannot eat all that is served.

I had deposited myself in a quiet unobtrusive nook to eat quietly, but at the same time amusing and indulging myself in watching people, my mind making the appropriate or inappropriate good-natured bitchy comments about the characters – large, small, homely, pretty and handsome or those in between. At least for me, it was better entertainment than dancing to hard rock Punjabi. It was at this moment when several of Ajay's blood-related aunties invited me to sit with them in a secluded section of the rooftop garden; they too were escapees from the loud music.

I had met Aunty Mayla before the wedding when we delivered the wedding invitation. She lived in a splendid three-story Indian house with roof space for living. The most striking part of her house was the swirling white and beige genuine marble floor. Her real pride and joy was the orange tree, growing many sweet oranges, squeezing fresh orange juice, "only for Australian guests," she smiled with her very white teeth. Aunty Mayla had style and grace, suggesting we all have an afternoon at the Amritsar Museum followed by a dinner. They were a cultured people in every sense of the word. We also met some friendly and funny extended family aunties, a mini version of the American comedienne Lucille Ball.

Then there was aunty Bendina, lovely and friendly, greeting Ajay for all to hear with a, "My god, you have grown! It seems only yesterday when you were wetting your pants." Turning to Darius she said, "And you, omg, hot-hot! How many girls have you westerners roomed around with", turning again to Ajay, having just kissed him but his slight beard bothering her, she got on to it, "why haven't you shaved? Now that Jag is married, we will organize a girl for you. Jag took a long time to find a good woman, but we will help you fast track your romance and marriage." Looking at me she said, "You better save your money because there will be another wedding soon."

In Australia, many of the younger Indians call Indians who are older 'Aunty' or 'Uncle'. The upwardly mobile Indians use it as a marker, but there is no blood relation. Many Indians don't like being called 'aunty' or 'uncle' as it is often used as a type of derogatory remark of a doting busybody or old codgers.

The safest way is not to call people 'aunty'; just ask what their names are. Ajay says only call them 'aunties' if they are part of your family. Many younger Indians use the term 'aunty' as a form of antagonism. Calling younger women 'aunty' is not very nice.

Believe it or not, we were introduced to Aunty Mame. She loved it when we spontaneously sang "you coax the blues right out of the horn, Mame; you charm the husk right of the corn, Mame. You've got the banjos strumming. You've made us feel alive again; you've made us feel alive again. You've given us the drive again." The song 'Mame' was written by Jerry Herman and made famous by Louis Armstrong.

Some aunties' curiosity astounds me, in a humorous way I hasten to say, because they keep asking busybody questions, probably because their own lives are lacking romance, desire and love so everything is projected on their objects of love, usually their own handsome younger nephews. Such was the case with Ajay, hence, the interest in his private life back in Australia. Turning to me, speaking loudly so everybody could hear, but still being pleasant, pleasant enough yet bordering on annoyance saying, "Tell us about Ajay's girlfriends. Does he have many, are they pretty, does he ever talk about marriage, and what is his house like?" This particular aunt has a *ritsha* for everybody. It seems she had marriage plans on her mind even asking me if there was anyone special in my life. She has an Indian girl in mind for me she says. Who needs social media, muses Darius when we have an in-house walking matrimonial site.

Another extended family aunty gives us unasked advice about house cleaning, cooking, and raising children. She is also the drama aunty making a scene out of everything! She can complain about anything in the same way the paneer was not done right. She hugs you and cries when someone disagrees with her or gets upset when someone forgets to say hi to her. Attention is her drug, and always dramas, her way out of awkwardness. Well, you cannot escape them, and each one of them has their own unique way of burning your ears and soul. Life would not be the same in India without the aunties. They bring much-needed drama and diversion in our often boring lives.

Ro, the fruit Juice man, a recent IT Graduate, his whole appearance was carefully groomed, and like most Indian men, he had perfect white teeth, tall and athletic, not inclined to slothfulness having the kind of demeanour that said, "At one with the universe". He had an unprejudiced enquiring mind, our eyes met and again we realized that our past had met the present.

CHAPTER 13

SHE FEELS LIKE AN INDIAN LIGHT BEAM WHEN SHE DOES SOCIAL MEDIA

Darius was suffering from some kind of stomach wog. The Dr diagnosed the infamous *Giardiasis parasite.* Annoying, but not to worry, the doctor said it doesn't get into the bloodstream. Only four tablets were prescribed to be taken all at once; these would destroy the parasites almost immediately stopping the annoying runs and the accompanying debilitating dehydration. He probably caught the stomach parasite in a swimming hole alongside the fast-flowing Beas River, or maybe the ice-cream he was given afterwards by his bodybuilding fans at the gym or perhaps he cleaned his teeth with risky ordinary tap water. They warn you about all of the risks in the tourist brochures, "You westerners are so weak, you catch anything," laughed Ajay.

Right now we are in the small bustling Punjabi city of Kartarpur sauntering amongst the Wallahs (vendors) observing lively street scenes, enjoying the streets bustling with social and economic activity, artists, jewellery and textile designers, flour millers, goldsmiths and their foundries, gold and precious stone dealers, panel beaters, motor repairers, booksellers, food shops selling delicatessen of every imagination dispensed from family stalls, moving carts, or pop up shops. The language one hears on the streets is of trading, exchanging currency, contracting deals, negotiating prices, buying and selling, not to mention the whirling spinning wheels weaving multi-coloured designer-inspired clothes showing motifs of ancient and modern India.

Someone is calling out to us, "uthe sanadara dosata hana" immediately followed by an English translation, "hi there handsome friends." I follow Darius to one of the El Fresco Fruit Juice Bar named "Juice Delight" where a tall, handsome Indian is bowing gracefully pointing and beckoning us to sit down into the kerbside vacant chairs, smilingly introducing himself as Ro, and his female assistant as Susah, a doppelganger of the famous Indian actress Anushka Sharma. All our senses are somewhat overwhelmed as we popped down in the seats taking in the fragrance of fresh fruit. Attracted by the inviting produce and friendly customer service by the delightful Juice Barman, who expertly and hygienically mixes the juices with crushed ice, blending the delicious raw mangoes and masala, an Indian mixture of various herbs poured into old jam jars with thick edges, never mind the type of containers at least they are recyclables as long as the content stops our dehydration. Waiting for the pour, we are astonished by the local cloth designs and their high-quality material in the textile shops while waiting for our second serve of fresh lemon, orange lime and soda mixed with salt and sugar juice squeezed out from the locally grown sugarcane. When Ro the fruit barman asks us why we did not bring our wives with us to India, then pausing, asking discreetly if we prefer men instead; silence. People seem, at times, to be obsessed about who one's partner is or who belongs to whom. Of course, neither Darius nor I or Ajay are married although Ajay's parents are working hard for him in getting a wife. "It's a destiny thing getting a wife for young Indians," Darius says while winking at Ro, "for us westerners, it's okay not to have a wife. Society does not keep hassling us, there is no pressure for us to get a wife, husband or any other partner; when you have a wife, you must have babies and the world is already grossly overpopulated. We really should not make any more babies, just adopt children that do not have families." In India it's different. However, we are careful not to self-disclose too much to mere acquaintances or to pursue that line of sensitive conversation when we are not on our own turf.

Yesterday, one of our Dutch friends called us telling us he was attacked when he paid with his rainbow-coloured *Bunq card* in Lucknow, a large city in Northern India not too far from where we were, saying after he had paid his bill, eight men started making derogatory and homophobic remarks and then attacked him. Our friend suffered serious lacerations to his face and head; he is now in hospital. This fitted in with the conversations about how much Social Media has impacted on Indian society. That would not happen to us, said Darius because we would quickly adopt an air of intimidation when we felt threatened, our body language saying don't mess with us had saved us from little nasties during our travels in India.

Ro, the fruit Juice man, a recent IT Graduate, his whole appearance was carefully groomed, and like most Indian men, he had perfect white teeth, tall and athletic, not inclined to slothfulness having the kind of demeanour that said, "At one with the universe". He had an unprejudiced enquiring mind, our eyes met and again we realized that our past had met the present.

More people joined our congenial conversation. They just sat next to us sharing a table and join in with the flow of whatever the topic of conversations, one of which was "how the internet has changed India"; what kind of social and cultural impacts are evident? Ro said that "due to social media, the impacts are phenomenal. It has turned the Indian village into a megapolis causing the biggest sea change since the advent of Gutenberg's moveable type. Every young Indian under thirty years of age is now a more global citizen, at least, secretly if not openly than an Indian citizen. The internet has given them a global mind and global urge diminishing their Indian cultural mindset."

"Yes," Susha says, "the proof of this is that we become much more individualistic like the west rather than the collectiveness we have in India. With the newly acquired global and individualistic mindset, millions of young Indians want to live in Europe, Australia, Canada, the USA or New Zealand." It also means that they have to conform to the norms and values of the prevailing cultures into which they want to settle, but due to socializing towards these western norms that would be no problem.

Fellow fruit juice drinker Sonia, a 24-year-old woman looking like an Indian version of Italian actress *Gina Lollobrigida*, simultaneously joins our conversation saying she feels like an Indian light beam when she does social media, "Everything I want is there, relationships, love, books, friends, music, and movies. I really don't need a car to get about, I haven't got one anyway, just an old Moped. Someone else asks how much are Indians thinking about their place in the world, especially the younger generation whose mind and changed habits have been shaped by the Internet information highway. The gaining of more information about other countries is a stimulus for Indians seeking adventure out of India: we smile because nearly every young Indian we meet asks us about getting them a visa or sponsor them to come to live or study in Australia.

Surprisingly, we find out that many Indian young people are members of virtual dating communities. Ro says, "Dating today is totally different than nineteen years ago, I can now find a wife on Tinder and don't need my parents anymore for the same."

I liked Ro's type of ironic humour saying that a large virtual community can be a double-edged sword, creating more possibilities for human misery as well as satisfaction. It has enlarged the social life of India by being connected to everyone on planet earth bringing more opportunities for cooperation and mutual benefits.

Ajay isn't so sure about this great chance even if it is for the better because some things will always stay the same such as human nature that has not changed since the Stone Age; love, hate, greed, jealousies, rivalries, thrill-seeking, pride, contempt, esteem and glory. Those negative aspects of human nature can only change through spirituality, not through the Internet. Yet, as Sonja said, "Human nature could change considering we all are living on the cusp of the third great tipping point in human history". Darius added that the tipping point is a point in time, a magic moment when an idea, trend or social behaviour is rapidly and often dramatically changing cultural behaviours by adopting previously rare practices. The term *Tipping Point* was defined by writer *Malcolm Gladwell.* That is true in India; politics and religion are wedded to various ethnic groups forming the nation. Since the Internet, nations such as India are slowly becoming detached from their cultures of origin, not due to the movement of people but through the world wide web of media-friendly information, new ideas and knowledge.

I laugh, so many of my Indian friends travelling on the train from Geelong to Melbourne used to tell me they were not vegetarian in Australia but only in India because they did not want to offend their culturally sensitive relatives who were not connected to the Internet and remained closed-minded to the ideas of the ever-changing world, believing that a connected world shrinks differences and divisions making the world a safer place. Of course, our Indians on our fruit juice table were highly intelligent and certainly not naïve. They all talked about the negative aspects of the WWW like religious fanatics showing how to make a bomb and certain organisations making up false news in order to sabotage truth and manufacture their own facts. However, we will leave this for another juice session, at least it gave us an insight into what India's ordinary people were thinking about; the impact of the internet. Nonetheless, we all agreed one thing – social media is slowly diminishing Indian culture through changing homogeneity the acceptance of diversity and the end of the ever controlling consensus and societal conformity.

CHAPTER 14

CAN YOU GET ME A VISA TO AUSTRALIA? DO YOU REALLY WANT TO GO THERE, OBLITERATING A FEW AUSTRALIAN STEREOTYPES

"Can you help me with a Visa and maybe a job in Australia?" This would have to be the most common question young Indian adults asked us; but why the obsession of going to Western Countries to study and work, what is wrong with India? A country so much more advanced on so many levels.

Like a chorus, they replied, "India is overpopulated, especially in the cities and provincial towns, and there are few jobs for graduates. Australia, a nation continent, and Canada still have enormous thinly populated spaces having room for millions more." I hesitated to tell that most of the Australian population lives in densely populated, polluted cities with as many traffic jams as New Delhi and Mumbai. Melbourne has a population of 5 million, Sydney 6 million, Perth 4 million as has Brisbane. Add all this up and 21 million Aussies live in densely populated areas and a mere 5 million are spread out all over the continent. In Australia, Indians usually settle in their own colonies such as Tarbeith and Wyndhamvale in the state of Victoria.

Yes, and there is a lot of resentment by ignorant xenophobic Australians who fear anything different from themselves. Some conservative right wing Nationalist Parties are against migrants, Muslims, Hindus and Gay people. Members of these parties are fiercely and irrationally nationalistic, often ignorant and psychotic.

The fruit juice bar conversations continued; this one, a few days later after our first conversations. Things in India often happened along footpaths such as this kerbside pop up fruit juice stall, where Ajay, myself and Darius made acquaintance with Ro, the young zestful entrepreneurial owner and operator of this funky Fruit Juice Bar serving exotic juices in used Jam Jars. Wherever we went, we seemed to draw unintentional attention to ourselves, maybe it was the clothes we wore, we did not want to look like Christian missionaries or looking like the US Americans, so we wore mostly smart European designed clothes not made in China. Ajay disagreed and jokingly said it was our vivacious characters and healthy looks that fascinated people. Many a thing spoken in jest, came to mind.

It only took a few glasses of mixed Mango Lemon juice for the other zippy Indian millennials to join our kerbside conversations, Sangee a pleasant and assertive sparkling enthusiastic woman spontaneously asking us how she could fix a move to either Canada or Australia to live and study. Like thousands of young Indian people, Sangee was seeking to break the monotony of what she saw as cultural restrictions, or was she looking for adventure, driven by a desire to make her own way in the world. Yet Sangee seemed culturally conservative wearing a sari including visible body piercings. Indicative of many Indians, her spoken English was perfect. We told them that their spoken English would put the average Australian to shame.

Ro wanted to move away from India because he desired to be his individualist self, being his own man, quoting Polonius in Shakespeare's Hamlets, "Know Thyself, or to thine own self be true and it must follow, as the night the day. Thou canst not then be false to any man." In India, he said, "I have to conform to cultural norms. I can't honestly be an atheist for example, not that I am an Atheist, I would be ostracized by my relatives, but in the west, I can be my authentic self. Don't get me wrong, I love India," he quickly added. Ro innocently believed that Indians have so much in common with Australians such as cricket and the English language, and driving on the left-hand side of the road. None of us was a cricket enthusiast. The majority of Australians do not play cricket and are only armchair enthusiasts. There was almost a look of disbelief when we said we were no fans of cricket. It's hardly a world game, seven countries in the world play the kind of test match cricket India does. There is no international cricket in Canada. Sadly, of late, Australian "rubbing the ball" cricketers are known for their cheating and arrogance.

A closer Indian tie to Australia would be that India has a part in the ANZAC Myth, sixteen thousand Indian troops fought alongside Australian and New Zealanders, aka ANZACS who invaded Turkey in 1915. The Spirit of the ANZAC Myth celebrated every 25th April with a holy reverence also belongs to India. The myth is about shared qualities – endurance, courage, ingenuity, good humour and mate-ship. These close ties between Australia and India are traced back to the landing at Anzac Cove. The Sikhs and Gurkhas lost 1600 men, Professor Peter Staley recently published the book *"Die in Battle Do not Despair, The Indians on Gallipoli."*

Sangee thought that Indians should easily be able to come to Australia by virtue of India being a part of the British Commonwealth Nations, wondering what this membership did for the individual Indian. This membership does not benefit the individual Indian one iota: You'll still need a Visa to travel to every Commonwealth country in the world without any benefits, not like the European Union (EU) whose citizens can work everywhere and travel freely without visas, should not the Commonwealth be like that? Ajay felt that the Commonwealth is still a racist and colonial organisation. The British Commonwealth does not mean a thing, seven of its member countries are at the top of Human Rights abusers in the world, with a reputation of brutal atrocities. Even in

Australia, Human Rights are dubious and not guaranteed, it being one of the few Western countries that did not have a Charter of Human Rights. Because Australia does not have a Charter Of human rights, it banishes refugees that come by boat for life without a criminal conviction to offshore detention camps such as Nauru and Manus, totally against the UN 1951 Convention on Refugees. You need to know that Australia's stand is condemned by the International community.

It was only in the mid-sixties that Australia dismantled her *White Australia Policy* and it took a good ten years to fully implement. It meant no coloured people were allowed to permanently settle in Australia, no mass Indian or Asian migration such as we thankfully have today. It was, in fact, a hidden apartheid policy. The white settlers only gave the indigenous people the vote in 1962, and in 1968 they changed the constitution through a referendum recognizing the original indigenous owners of the lands as equal with white people and that was done through a referendum to include them in the constitution.

Vishal, an Indian medical doctor and a friend of Sangee sat quietly listening to these conversations, chirped up relating his experiences in Australia as a medical intern experiencing discrimination at work especially in Hospitals, not from the staff but from backward uneducated white people who refused to be seen by an Indian doctor, bluntly demanding they wanted a white doctor. I recalled some Indian nurses at the Geelong Hospital also being discriminated against by the white settlers who demanded white nurses. Thankfully, the Hospital management stood up against this kind of discrimination and told the patient there was no choice and if they did not like it, they could go elsewhere for treatment.

There seems to be a view in India that Australia has no poverty such as in India. We Googled the statistic and showed several examples. Like India, Australia has widespread poverty,

35% of the 3 million Australian pensioners live below the poverty line and are the poorest in the OECD, another 1 million children live in poverty and we have half a million homeless people living rough camping in all our cities.

Religion in Australia gets special privileges and is allowed to blatantly discriminate under law. Religious Schools – Christian, Hindu, Muslim schools receive more tax payer's money than the Secular State Schools. Religions have special privileges; in that, they are exempt from the Country's *Equal Opportunity laws*. They can refuse jobs to divorced people and expel Gay, Lesbian Bisexual, Transgender students from schools. Secular organizations and employers are not allowed to discriminate on the basis of Race, Religion, Sexual Orientation, yet Religious people or organizations are given exemptions.

Mental health issues are a big problem in Australia. Suicide is the number one cause of death in the 15 to 24 age group, second in the 25 to 44 age group, and the third highest cause of death in the 45 to 64 age group. What does this tell you about Australian society?

In Australia, one does do not automatically get a pension; there is an assets test. Your Indian Old Age Pension, a non-contributory old-age pension scheme covers all Indian citizens who are 60 years and is given when you live below the poverty line. The difference is that in India, the cost of living is very low whereas Australia has one of the highest costs of living in the world. Food, rent and power charges keep ordinary people poor.

Ajay referred to my first book *Vertrek*, which created such intrigue of how we, post Second World War, Dutch people from The Netherlands suffered from cultural shock when we first came to Australia. I was glad to oblige and took my Indian friends through an imaginary journey into the migrant assimilation camps.

We were sent to Bonnegilla, a migrant transit assimilation camp situated 400 kilometres from Melbourne near Albury

Wodonga almost in the middle of nowhere near Lake Hume Weir. We arrived in the middle of the night, were disinfected and provided with Australian food including foul-smelling sheep meat called mutton, pumpkin and corn, considered pig food in The Netherlands, foods that were alien to Dutch people. The next day during orientation, we were given the rules of the camp; only speak English, speaking your own language was discouraged and speaking a foreign language other than English in public such as on trains, trams and buses was considered rude. My mother had to attend Australian cooking classes conducted by the Country Women's Association and was encouraged to prepare dinner of three vegs and a chop...too bad if you were vegetarian. For three weeks, everybody attended information sessions on Australian laws, norms and values. It was best to conform to all of these if you wanted to integrate successfully in Australian culture. On the second day, my mum spoke to the headmaster at the new primary school and told him not to hit me with a strap. If I was misbehaving, my parents would correct my behaviour, not the barbaric school teachers with their strap; we were never strapped as a consequence.

After being in Australia for six months, the police came to our home to arrest me for reading a banned book that my aunty from The Netherlands had sent me. The immigration brochures never told us that there was book censorship on literature like they had in the then Soviet Union or Communist China. We suffered a great deal from cultural shock. Indians migrating to Australia today usually do not suffer cultural shock as they are mostly absorbed in the Indian communities living in what seem designated areas such as Tarneith and Wyndhamvale in Victoria.

Clumping of migrant groups such as we now have in Australia was not encouraged. The white, blond, blue-eyed Dutch, English, Germans Scandinavian assimilated in the Australian community very quickly. The dark-skinned Greeks and Italians and Jews were very clannish and formed their own neighbourhoods as do the Indians, Chinese, Vietnamese and Iranians today.

Yes, and there is a lot of resentment by ignorant xenophobic Australians who fear anything different from themselves. Some conservative right wing Nationalist Parties are against migrants, Muslims Hindus and Gay people. Members of these parties are fiercely and irrationally nationalistic, often ignorant and psychotic.

Now we are truly multicultural and have learnt from our past mistakes. Considering all non-indigenous Australians came here from Europe as convicts, free settlers or migrants of one sort or another less than 250 years ago, the majority of Australian people are welcoming to all migrants; they are seen as making valuable contributions to the nation. Assimilation is no longer an issue as we are now multicultural. However, I am ashamed to say that our record on the treatment of indigenous people is nothing but scandalous and we should be ashamed as a nation. Health issues, employment, homelessness, incarceration are a big concern for indigenous communities. HIV AIDS in the north of Australia are now in plague proportions, but you would not know about it. The media in Australia is controlled by a few very right-wing bigoted old white men. The only middle of the road newspaper that actually still does investigative journalism is the Guardian.

Coming to Australia, you have to get used to things being run by privileged white men and a few women, who are mostly Anglophone, whose only reference to the world is Canada, New Zealand, the USA, and Britain. A few of these white men speak any foreign languages; this is especially true of the conservative LNP Government members and their Prime Minister who mixes his personal faux Christian religion with his political ideology.

There is corruption in Australia just as there is in India. Recently we had *A Royal Commission into the Banking Sector* and the outcomes were not pretty showing corruption, dishonesty, and nepotism, money laundering, lying and ripping off customers' billions of dollars. Then there was *the Royal Commission into Institutional Child Abuse,* this took five years of investigation and the outcomes were horrific tales of child abuse mainly in Religious Institutions and in Australia's armed forces and in Government schools. As I write this, yet another *Royal Commission into Aged Care* is showing the corruption, negligence of how older citizens are being neglected, then compare this with the respect and reverence senior citizens are treated in India.

"What about the beggars and homeless in India?" Sue asks. "What did you see in Melbourne this morning, Sue?" "Well, yes, hundreds of people sleeping rough under the awnings of shops in Bourke, Swanston, Elizabeth street not to mention the hundred or so sleeping in treasury gardens and so many begging for money and food in all Australian cities. So what about the homeless and beggars in India?"

CHAPTER 15

COMPARISONS ARE ODIOUS

Comparisons often come from a biased conscience filled with stereotypical ideas and can be misleading perpetuated by people who are usually not well-read, having few critical thinking skills, easily influenced by mainstream media. Asking questions of comparison can sometimes be an indication of hiding behind an air of racial or nationalistic superiority, such as my Australian friends Sue and Bob.

Before travelling to India, I was given plenty of stereotypical advice such as, watch out for pickpockets, Indian car drivers are like kamikaze suicide drivers, don't catch Delhi Belly, Indians are snake charmers, and they don't use toilet paper. Indians wobble their heads and you don't know which way to turn as it is either yes or no.

In preparing ourselves for India, we watched many documentaries and films such as *Slumdog Millionaire*, that's the real India they said. *The Best Exotic Marigold Hotel* showed the chaos and different ways of doing business, were an untruth, is just a different perspective, and life and love can only begin in India if you let go off your western past. As soon as we arrived in India, we posted pictures on Facebook about our first impressions. Like boys in a toyshop, these pictures were brimming with enthusiasm. Several of my readers and friends did not like the positive things we had observed about India, disappointed because we wrote nothing about the rapes of women, or about poverty, the homeless, the beggars, the bribery in bureaucracy and government corruption, not to mention the filth on the streets, the superstitious nature of Indians, the constant oppressive heat, pollution and the environment. Our pictures and comments did not reinforce their negative stereotypical images of India. Consequently, several Facebook friends unfriended me, evidence that my favourable impressions caused a war on social media. Because my "perception is reality", my positive posts smashed their biased stereotyped images of this ancient land.

The aforementioned Sue and her husband Bob, both conservative voters and proud of their Australian convict heritage were critical of my positive reports. I wasn't surprised their Anglo narrow minds, as opposed to the global broad mind, were fed and programmed by the *Daily Telegraph*, owned by Media Mogul Rupert Murdoch, and salacious women's gossip magazines. They only watch commercial TV channels, and do not watch the ABC; in Sue's opinion, it's full of lefties, and they can't stand the "woggy" multicultural SBS TV station, "They are so un-Australian," as she puts it. Their knowledge of Australian History is well, she says, "James Cook discovered Australia, and when the English landed in 1783, the continent was virtually empty." Bob thinks that Aboriginals are good for nothing saying they have drinking problems. Sue and her Bob are fearful people, she picks up her kids from school in a big SUV, one of those with a menacing oversized robust "kangaroo" bumper bar. She is an aggressive driver as she beats other mothers to empty parking spots when she picks up her two kids even though she only lives a 15-minute-walk away from school. She trusts little, hence her fear of "stranger danger" a paranoid fear of strangers, being afraid of Asians, Muslims. Sue and Bob determinately fought against same-sex marriage. They are enthusiastic members of the Anglican Diocese of Sydney proud that their Diocese spends one million Australian dollars against the recent plebiscite on same-sex-marriage and equality. They're keen supporters of Australia's Christian Prime Minister who, for six years, operated and continues to operate Australia's gulag of detention camps.

On Nauru and Manus Islands are thousands of innocent refugees treated by Australia as criminals. Without having a court trial to decide if they have broken any laws, the Australian government says these refugees are criminals. Sue does not know what the word xenophobic implies; they believe Australia should reduce its migrant intake especially Indian, Chinese and Muslims, almost suggesting we should go back to the homogeneous *White Australia Policy which* they view as the golden years of Australia; plenty of jobs for everyone, less crowded cities, and only one language. Despite her views, we are still friends, me voting for *Groen Links* (Left Green) in Nederland, they like the Dutch because they look so much like Australians. Australians, to me, look like humans. Are Sue and Bob typical Australians? Thank God, no!

It was Sue and her Netball girlfriends who caused such a song and dance about our India postings "what about all the rapes in India?" Our answer was "What about all the rapes in Australia? We are fourth in the world for rapes and domestic violence and alcohol consumption. And for Australia being a safe place, during the last six months, 36 Australian women have been murdered on the streets while going home or murdered in their own homes. Indian women are no more suppressed than Australian women who got the vote in 1962. Prior to this, only white Australian women got the vote. All Indian women got the vote in India in 1947 regardless of race or caste. In several Indian states, property names and wealth passes from mother to daughter rather than father to son.

"What about the beggars and homeless in India?" Sue asks. "What did you see in Melbourne this morning, Sue?"

"Well, yes, hundreds of people sleeping rough under the awnings of shops in Bourke, Swanston, Elizabeth street not to mention the hundred or so sleeping in treasury gardens and so many begging for money and food in all Australian cities. So what about the homeless and beggars in India?"

Just then Bill, Sue's husband, a businessman, asks "And what about the culture of corruption and bribery in India?"

"What about it Bill? Can you recall the recent *Australian Royal Commission into the Banks* and its final conclusion that the Major Banks in Australia were corrupt to their core?" Bill went quiet; he realized that throwing negative stereotypes at India bounced right back to Australia. "What about Child brides and child abuse?" Sue said, not realizing that not too many years ago in Australia, a twelve-year-old girl could marry. Sue was embarrassed about the recent *Royal Commission into Institutional Child Abuse* especially by religious organizations like your Anglican Diocese. The Commission sat for five years, interviewed more than 8000 child victims and published 17 volumes. 92% of the victims suffered under the watch of Christian organizations and not one victim from either an Islamic Mosque or a Hindu Temple, so let us not compare ourselves with India, we come off worse every time. Indian families usually do not dump their senior citizens in nursing homes as we do in the west. Take *The Royal Commission into the care of Nursing homes* for the elderly, revelations coming forth are beyond telling. In India, older people are actually venerated, honoured and respected, there is no ageism to speak of. In Australia, we cannot wait soon enough to plunk our elderly, who are venerated for their dollar not their wisdom and contribution to society in moneymaking shareholders driven Aged Care."

Sue's many adverse stereotypic attitude were gained from Anglo tabloids and from Television shows such as the popular

British comedy sitcom *'Kumar at number 42'* guilty of promoting popular stereotypes. In reality, the Kumar's are not typical Indians as Australia's *'Kath and Kim' or Dame Edna Everage,* are not representative of Australian women. Sue got upset when I inferred Kath and Kim talked like her with a typical Australian upward inflexion making them sound like a trumpet, and then there is *Bart Simpson* where all 7/11 shops are owned by accented Indians. No doubt these negative images have been programmed and stored in her subconscious mind, coming to the fore when she is defending her "superior western and in particular Australian white culture".

"Yes, but the Indian toilets," she cringes.

"What about Indian toilets? I found them everywhere, with toilet paper too and the Indian Government is placing 7.5 million new toilets in the next five years, that's 700 toilets each day! By comparison, public toilets in Australia are diminishing; instead, we are encouraged to go behind trees or in isolated corners of laneways in our cities," I chuckle.

Indian society is not as conservative as portrayed by the Indian mainstream media. I had just received a Facebook post from Krishna, who participated in the Amritsar First Ever - Gay Pride Parade. He said 75 joined the march but a thousand joined the party afterwards. Most marchers were wearing face paint and carrying rainbow pride flags and it was the first parade in Punjab. They assembled at the Rose Garden where he met his Banker, Ravinder S who objected to GLBTIQ people being so public and in your face. Krishna, ever quick of the mark said, "Well Ravinder, if you were outside of Punjab, say in Australia or Canada, and people told you they thought it offensive for you to wear your turban and throwing your Sikh Religion and your straight sexual orientation into their faces, how would you feel?" Silence by Ravinder; point taken.

For all its disadvantages social media is a great education tool bringing people together with shared experiences.

I continued to post my positive impressions destroying Indian myths and stereotypical images such as – There is no general dowry for Indian brides. Not all Indians live in large extended families. Indians are not uncomfortable with interacting with the opposite sex. Not all Indians are vegetarians, it is a choice what one eats, India is the largest beef exporter in the world exporting more beef than Australia does. Cricket is not the religion of every Indian; tennis, badminton and football are also popular. All educated Indians are not IT professionals; only 1 out of every 200.

CHAPTER 16

THE GOLDEN TEMPLE IN AMRISTAR

A magic realism hangs around the Temple even when we arrived at 10 pm. Outside the Temple, a carnival atmosphere prevailed, yet one sensed a holy purity. Everything was extremely clean, not a piece of paper or plastic rubbish anywhere. The merchants' products outside the Temple had price tags, discouraging them in their usual price haggling. The food stalls were not all selling typical Indian food but take away Italian Pasta and Vietnamese noodles, all vegetarian, no dead flesh around the sacred Temple complex. No spilling of blood or sacrificial killing of sentient animals. Before entering the temple complex, we bought some sandalwood beads necklaces and Om armbands; they look good and make you feel a bit holy and the fragrance of the musky sandalwood enhances masculinity and keeps away annoying insects.

Darshan being the wisest and elder, whose family had been coming to The Golden Temple since he was a baby seven decades ago led us through the entry gate dedicated to Christ as a Christian; I was touched. There are four large gates each looking like a mini version of *Arc de Triomphe* in Paris, apparently dedicated to the four religious personages, Christ, Mohammed, Buddha and Lord Krishna. Before entering the temple complex, we had to purchase some orange bandanas to

As an amateur historian, I drew parallels with history and religion and philosophies; this helps me to understand human nature. I wondered why holy places around the world have such violent pasts, did they become holy places like memorials because so much blood had been shed.

cover our heads for the same reasons Sikhs and Jews wear their Kippah and Turban as a recognition that there is "someone above them" and to take care of their long hair and promote equality including to preserve their identity. There were special places to put out your shoes and disinfect your naked feet by walking through a channel of warm water. Sikhs consider footwear dirty and unworthy of entering a house, let alone a Temple such as the premier Golden Temple. We also had to change our shorts to long pants, many Indians consider naked male legs erotic and indecent in public, certainly at this temple. Darshan explained that the Golden Temple proper, a gold plated building placed in the middle of the lake is plated with Gold and is the holiest place for Sikhs who call the temple *Sri Harmandir Sahib,* meaning the "abode of God".

It was built around a manmade lake completed by Guru Ram Das in 1577 (compare this with St Peter's Basilica in Rome, it began in 1506 and finished in 1626), but was frequently destroyed and rebuilt by the Sikhs. The Golden Temple's architecture is a mixture of Indo Islamic and Mughal Hindu Raj. It has such a mixture of style because it was destroyed and rebuilt so many times.

The Temple contains the Sikh Holy Book called the Adi *Granth,* which is on display for 18 hours and then is literally put to bed. Krishna took us in the bedroom to have a look, and lo, yes, the *Adi Granth* was put to bed in an 18th-century English-like bed and covered with a blanket. Of course, we knew about the Golden Temple back in 1980 when Prime Minister Indira Gandhi ordered an invasion on the Golden Temple because a Sikh separatist movement had taken up headquarters there. Under Operation Blue Star, Indira ordered an attack on the Golden Temple resulting in the deaths of thousands of soldiers and civilian Sikh independence fighters. "Yes," Darshan said, "the payback was when her Sikh bodyguards murdered her, The Prime Minister, in her own home."

We finally entered through the gates dedicated to Christ. It was just a very big Arch, big enough for tanks and trucks to pass through, not too many decorations of carvings, yet modest in ornamentals. Starting our walk around the peripheral of the Golden Temple lake called the *Holy parikrama,* not unlike the station of the cross in Catholic Churches. Krishna pointed out an ancient tree called the *Dukh Bhanjani Ber Tree;* they said that the leaves have the power to cure any ailments and free people of all worries and sorrows. Jokingly, Darius said they should plant trees like this in Australia as the Aussies take more anti-psychotic tablets for worry and depression than any nation on earth and drown their sorrows with alcohol. This tree would indeed be a blessing even though they often carried this melancholy of Indian mysticism with them; Darius found this mysticism intrigued because it seems more like playfulness with our emotions, there was a lot of nuances attached to this spiritual mysticism.

Not far from here was another massacre memorial caused deliberately by the British on 20 April 1919 under the command of British General Dyer, a Christian, responsible for the Amritsar massacre near *Jallianwala Bagh* ten minutes away from the Golden Temple. Dyer shot fifteen hundred Indians in cold blood. Listening to this horror story and viewing the names of those people shot, I could still feel the Indian bitterness against the British. Maybe this is why my Indian hosts and friends encouraged us to wear Indian traditional male wear so we did not look too western and certainly not Christian.

As an amateur historian, I drew parallels with history and religion and philosophies; this helps me to understand human nature. I wondered why holy places around the world have such violent pasts, did they become holy places like memorials because so much blood had been shed. Look at Jerusalem, the Wailing Wall and the Dome of The Rock on the place where God audibly asks Abraham to sacrifice his son Isaac on Mount

Moriah, and the exact place where the Prophet Muhammad, founder of Islam, is believed to have ascended into heaven. Rome and St Peter's Basilica were financed through the sale of indulgences, meaning people would give the Roman Catholic Church money, lots of it and this would reduce their time in Hell. The sales of indulgences were one of the causes why the Protestant Reformation happened, always the spilling of blood and more innocent blood. "Oh yes, but Rome is nothing compared with the Golden Temple," Darius explained, "here we have in the Temple complex one hundred thousand people visiting each day alone and wait for it, they all get fed a very nutritious vegetarian meal 24 hours per day to all people without any discrimination and no cost. Can you imagine the Roman Catholic Church in Rome providing meals to all the tourist visitors? It isn't happening! Well, in India, at The Golden Temple, this is possible, and then, nota bene there is morning and afternoon, evening and night Chai being served around the clock. Now they also have tea without sugar for those with diabetes."

There were several ceremonies. They consider their scripture as a living person because it is a living Logo, the word of God. We were very privileged to attend the closing rituals called *suskhasan* which mean putting to rest the holy book *Adi Granth and* carry it on a flower-decorated pillow accompanied by singing into the bedroom. The Bible is also called the Logo living word.

Both Darius and Krishna decided to take a dip in the lake surrounding the Golden Temple as many people believed the water has some sort of miraculous healing power. There were special areas for dressing and undressing. I waited outside and gave the very large sacred golden fishes some leftover holy food whereupon a guard dressed in Blue and a Yellow Turban nicely asked me to please not feed the fish, and to sit down crossed legged while waiting for my friends to finish their holy dip...the water was crystal clear, being purified constantly by hundreds of volunteers: a few leaves dropped on my head when I suddenly realized I was sitting under the *Dukh Bhanjani Ber Tree* with its miraculous healing leaves against worry and depression, some leaves had dropped off. I saved these leaves and surreptitiously put some into my pocket. I was struck by awe as I realized I was sitting under the sacred tree where Kim Das had sat under supervising the work over 400 years ago.

CHAPTER 17

TRAIN JOURNEYS, AND DIWALI FESTIVAL

A visit to India is never complete without a train journey. I wanted this experience ever since I was a child. They say one has not experienced India if you have not travelled third class on an Indian train. I read an account of Mahatma Gandhi about his train journey from Mumbai to Jaipur. He travelled third class and listed its shortcoming much more direct to what I would say, but the third class was not all that different from third class travel in India 100 years ago. It made me prepared and I was looking forward to the experience of a type of colonial train travel.

We had to travel back to New Delhi to get our wedding costumes measured and fitted for the wedding, catching the first class train from Beas to New Delhi leaving at 4 am for an 11 am appointment with the friendly Muslim tailors.

Travelling back to Beas was a different story because First Class was booked out so now we had to travel Third Class; 12-hour journey back to Beas because every other train had been booked out. In the morning we had travelled by a First Class Express train that cost 2000 rupees for an eight-hour journey. But the late-night train to Amritsar was Third Class and the fare was 300 rupees. For that amount, I got an experience of a lifetime; the four of us were crammed into a

The oppressive heat became stifling, almost unbearable, the air conditioning or cooling system wasn't coping due to 40 people squeezing in a compartment made to hold only 22 people, it was difficult to breathe and there was lots of couching and sneezing. The small and hungry-looking toddlers and young children in my carriage had, I am sure, never seen a white face before.

sleeping apartment, three Bunk Beds on top of each other, it was difficult to sit up if you were tall. The throng of travellers pushing, squeezing forcing themselves into the train and into our sleeping berths was unbelievable. They came in through doors, the skinny passengers squeezed themselves through the bars in the windows. The magnitude of squeezing caused me to become separated from Darius and Krishna. They managed to share a Bunk, but the Bunk allocated to me was already occupied by four other people who did not speak English. We had, in fact, caught the Pilgrim train. Thousands and thousands of Pilgrims were on their way to Amritsar for a holy festival. Most of them had boarded at Mumbai. They were darker, shorter, thinner type of Indians, than the Punjabis. More of the pilgrims pushed themselves into the apartment; the consolation was that most of them had friendly, very dark eyes.

Momentarily, I felt isolated and lonely and everything seemed quite intimidating as people kept looking at me and pointing at my bag full of apples I had purchased at a Delhi Fresh fruit market. The oppressive heat became stifling, almost unbearable, the air conditioning or cooling system wasn't coping due to 40 people squeezing in a compartment made to hold only 22 people, it was difficult to breathe and there was lots of couching and sneezing. The small and hungry-looking toddlers and young children in my carriage had, I am sure, never seen a white face before. I felt like I was packed in a Nazi train on its way to a death camp. The heat and no personal space was unbearable, the children started to cry, frightened when looking at me. I had to do something to change this situation. Another eight hours of travelling to go. I was getting prickly and angry at losing Darius and Krishna in the melee to scramble on this train. This third-class train was a slow coach train stopping at every station. Once stopped, people rushed and scrambled for the urinal and bathrooms, because the one toilet in my carriage was overflowing. I had a large plastic bottle in a brown bag for urinal purposes with me. Each stop was a repeat of the previous; young Pilgrim men, slim, pliable and quick climbing and squeezing through the non-barred emergency windows some' of them forcing their way into the reserved second class carriage.

Focusing on two young, guessing to be six-year-old boys, sitting on their mum and dad's lap, I smiled and asked if they spoke English. They did albeit heavily accented and a little shy, "Would you like some nuts and an apple?" Big smiles all around the three kilos of almonds sultanas and the apples caused much happiness when I shared these around. These people, in my view, looked so poor and undernourished as though they had not eaten since they left Mumbai 12 hours ago. For self-preservation, I decided to share all of the apples cutting them in half gaining thirty pieces of half apples; that's how many people were in the carriage. My act of giving was met with kindness. It paid off, they could see me sweating and hot; they made a place for me at the window, the open window. Actually, after two hours, people became even more friendly as I showed some of the *Diwali* celebration sweets I had bought, I would share them with the people around me.

There were two Hijras in my carriage; they took half an apple and some almond nuts and blessed me. Apparently, it is common for them to travel third class to offer blessings and other quick personal services. Some are genuine Hijras and others are not.

Diwali held in mid-October or Mid-November coincides with the darkest night in India. They still use the Gregorian calendar for the festival is a multi-religious festival celebrated especially by Hindus, Sikhs and Jains as a festival of light, not unlike Hanukkah or Christmas. Celebrated as a spiritual victory of light over darkness and good over evil, knowledge over ignorance. Diwali like Christmas is also the major shopping period in India. Many people purchase new clothing and use it as a means to renew their relationships and social networks. Fireworks are a major expense. The fireworks did contribute to air pollution; a haze hung over Amritsar and Beas, but that is the price. Sitting on the rooftop with candles looking over Beas, the whole town is lit up in candles or small, fragrant oil lamps. The homes are warmed up by the gentle, whimpering light of the candles. Little children offer sweets and smiles. We dressed in our finest clothes.

I have been to several Diwali parties in Australia put on by Indian friends. Darius and I attended local festivities; it was a lot of fun, in fact, it was so much more fun than Christmas time in Australia punctuated by the mass slaughter of Animals and the enormous drinking of alcohol. Diwali is the opposite – no alcohol and no slaughter and eating and drinking of blood at Christmas time. The gifts too are different for Diwali, not so much materialistic but more food for the soul and spirit. Alcohol raises the spirit at Christmas time but human empathy in Diwali.

Which NATIONALITY do you LOOK LIKE?

Keith, you look...

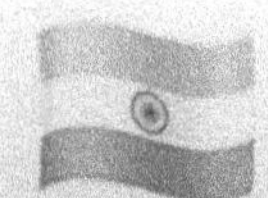

Indian

Prosperity said that in my past life, I was an Indian...and that I should be an Indian.
We had landed in the right place, the Ayurvedic Yoga Massage Life style Centre, where we were about to experience 4500 years of ancient health rituals emphasizing the way to physical beauty and spirituality through massage and bathing practice.

CHAPTER 18

THE HEAD MASSEUR INTRODUCED HIMSELF AS 'PROSPERITY' BECAUSE EVERYTHING HE TOUCHED PROSPERED

We had landed in the right place, the Ayurvedic Yoga Massage Lifestyle Centre, where we were about to experience 4500 years of ancient health rituals emphasizing the way to physical beauty and spirituality through massage and bathing practice. Situated in a Greco-Buddhist designed 700-year-old Temple similar to the famous Hammas male health spas in the Middle East. There were three designated spaces in the centre, the body area, the sacred knowledge area, and the spiritual meditation sanctuary garden. Little did we realize that we were now entering the Hindu world with its many parallel universes.

The all-white marble massage bathing rooms gave a peaceful and relaxed Zen feeling. The attractive yet austere simplicity broken up by the magnificent Indian friezes chiselled into the marble were Hindu, Buddhist, Greco motifs cut into the marble.

Masseurs wrapped soft white cotton towelettes around our half-naked gleaning bodies relaxing on warm marble slabs while sipping Soma nectar, the ritual drink of the Vedic Gods.

These very ancient yet modern massage techniques and deep relaxation reinvigorated us. Every muscle fibre was manipulated, veins and capillaries unblocked, stimulated by a period of deep breathing; like metamorphosis, a whole new creation emerged of spirit, mind and body. Relaxing herbal aromatic herbal oils made from recipes prescribed in the ancient Vedic text, geranium, frankincense, coriander, sweet almond, Jojoba oils were used on our skin to make it smooth. It felt more like a facial but all over the body exfoliating dead skin. The altering of our state of consciousness was happening; Darius's skin and whole body felt sensuously scintillating, not unlike Amyl Nitrate effect on skin and veins, he had taken at the western health spas, at least that is how the massages affected him, no doubt the Soma liqueurs were stimulating many of our senses. Amyl Nitrate was used as a medicine for people suffering from Angina, it relaxes the veins so the blood flows more freely and hence, it is used by masseurs to help relax muscles.

The head masseur introduced himself as *Prosperity* because everything he touched prospered. Krishna had met Prosperity before and now, here again, Prosperity had somehow surfaced or travelled from his unconscious mind to the conscious world. In a previous life, Krishna had loved Prosperity like Lord Krishna loved Arjuna, the devoted Vedic warrior pair. The Hindu books state that nobody in the whole world is dearer to Lord Krishna than Arjuna and would sacrifice anything, even his sons and wives. He loved him more than anything else. Oh, I had heard such parallels before, it sounded like a mirror relationship of David and Jonathan in the Bible, the love for each other surpassed the love of a woman.

Prosperity looked like a Greco Punjabi possessing desirable personality traits like enthusiasm, adaptability, patience humility, confidence, self-control, honesty and loyalty tied to some other interesting characteristics. One could call him extrovert, but that may not be right; he was equally introvert and besides, why should we label this beautiful Indian with a western psychological personality label. Showing a very fit and smooth hairless body, removed he said by a laser hair removal machine, the bottle-blond locks through his hair could easily make him model material for the Paris catwalk. He'd earn a good living with his exotic looks, not that Indians see him like this, but our western minds did.

He took us into the *sacred knowledge room* where some incense sticks were burning and some males singing *shabads*, other-worldly ancient tunes thousands of years old praising the Gods of nature. Prosperity showed us a copy of an ancient book called the *Sushruta Samhita*, a compilation of Ayurveda medical works containing instructions and methods about cataract surgery, lithotomy, treatment of anal and vaginal fistulas, mending fractures, amputations, caesarean births, "But! Plastic surgery topped the list," Prosperity said, and made people beautiful especially for repairing burnt or disfigured faces. European doctors from Italy, Spain, and England would come to India 300 odd years ago to learn surgeries such as a facelift and he said a westerner *Doctor Joseph Constantine Carpu* studied plastic surgery techniques in India for 20 years and then introduced it to Europe in 1815.

Prosperity was the archetype and image of Arjuna, which made it more awesome to listen to him. I asked where he had learned Ayurvedic medicine. He said he had read and meditated much and through these was given extraordinary spiritual insights and true-life experiences. "It's in my genes," he said, "lying dormant until ignited by an electronic wave hitting or awakening my unconscious becoming conscious, a gift from the Gods, shall we say?"

After the massages, light invigorating foods were served, not unlike Spanish tapas. The same pure chemical-free herbivorous foods that Lord Krishna and Arjuna consumed making them strong species of masculinity without spilling the blood of innocent animals. Prosperity told us that the sacred book, the "Rig Veda" (1700 BC 1100BC 1.017), contained ten books of sacred messages; spiritual, of health and healing besides historical fragments of the Aryan peoples and their enemies, the Dasas.

Parallels of religions and universes all have the same effect, in the end, the dethroning of humankind to something much greater. Hindu mythology has an infinite number of universes. In it, there is not one dilemma of modern man that has not existed before, especially in the body, mind and spirit realms. Problems change for each generation of humans, but in the end, what has been, will be again, what has been done again, "there is nothing new under the sun" spoken by the Ancient Hebrew King Solomon.

From the Rig Veda, we learnt that *Indra,* also known as *Vishnu* or Zeus, his Greek equivalent, was the supreme one God, the liberator of cows. There are definite parallels of the world's religions. Hinduism is as monotheistic as Christianity; it worships many avatars who perform many functions, sort of like CEOs in multinational companies. Christianity has Jehovah God, and his son Jesus Christ an incarnated avatar functioning as the Saviour of the world who, in turn, has millions of Avatars, good guardian angels at his disposal. The Holy Spirit, the third person of the God of Christianity, represents the invisible Jesus Christ on earth today. Then there is Satan with millions of evil avatars fighting for supremacy against the Jesus avatar angels. "But," quipped Darius, "these good guardian angels are often negligent of duty seemingly sleeping on the job as evidenced by the millions of children, men and women pleading for their lives in the Nazi concentration camps during World War Two, and guardian angels not intervening and neglectful of duty to the thousands of school children shot in the US."

The counter partner to Lucifer in Hindu is *Kalki Purana,* the source of all evil. Satan like *Kalki Purana* has his avatars wandering the earth giving out evil energy to vulnerable human beings.

Several young men join us in the sacred knowledge area after their body massages, one of whom, Rajeev (whose name means Blue Lotus) is a Quantum Physicist from *Jawaharial Nehru University* sharing his knowledge about unseen tiny objects that exist in multiple places and different states simultaneously. "There are so many things we cannot see," Rajeev says, "that are active all around us, such as electricity, radio waves that our brains send out triggering the neurons in our brain." Rajeev smiles and says, "Maybe the brain is just a computer that runs the program of our consciousness. What is thought? Or consciousness? Can you put these under a microscope and examine them? You cannot put a thought in a Petri dish under a microscope and examine it, can you?"

Rajeev likes to deepen our insights about the law of attraction having the ability to attract into our lives, whatever we are focusing on. In basic terms, our thoughts turn things into reality, eventually. He says that photons, electrons, and wave particles emitted from our brain make up the universe, convincingly saying that reality is what we choose; if we focus on negative doom and gloom, an individual will remain under that cloud. He quotes the ancient spiritual and scientific Vedic literature backing up his quantum physics theory. If we focus on positive thoughts and have goals that we aim to achieve, we will find a way to achieve them. '*Where there is a will, there is a way*'.

In India, the fantastic and the rich combine, it's magic realism, not much hypocrisy, but much authenticity especially at the *Satsangs* where we make friends with hundreds of friendly, highly intelligent people. All have something to say of substance, not the kind of superficiality and false diplomacy that the west is associated with. The Indians we met at the Ayurvedic Yoga Massage Lifestyle Centre had an ability to look deep into the human heart and soul, yet they had a fantastic style of humour. They believed that the present was what the past had produced yet giving a positive voice to the future.

Sipping more tea in the portico of the meditation sanctuary garden before we meditate, Prosperity emphasizes the finer points of meditation to suit the western mind. He said that meditation is not a religion, however, many people confuse the two. I agree and have found meditation to be extremely useful and wish I'd thought the many benefits when I was young. One problem in the west is that people confuse it with religion. To me, it's very opposite for it unites and does not divide us. We all have been given the ability to obtain peace within, peace of mind and peaceful hearts. Teaching children this at a young age would have huge benefits to them, and is validated by neuroscience.

Krishna introduces us to this 103 years old *Babaji* and wise Avatar, who has turned up from the Radha Soami community Satsang in Beas. He came to the centre riding a white stallion. This man only looks a sprightly fifty years old, clear skin and not yet depleted of collagen, muscles not degraded and blushing with energy and health. I ask him what his secret to such a healthy sharp mind is. He says, "Not criticizing people. We are well aware of their shortcomings but always find their positives virtues, every soul contains some virtue because God or nature is situated in every human heart." Then he quickly adds that being a lifelong non-violent vegetarian helps too. In the *Dera Satsangs,* there is no damaging dogma, as there are in Christianity. The old *Babaji* recons dogma causes war, division and exclusiveness. No condemnation in his Dera or telling people how to live, the only sermon is a walking one. This is true always when people look at a person that practices at remaining healthy, working at looking good, practising unconditional love to all. Babaji says, "It's like your Christ who said 'if he was lifted up, all men and women would be drawn to love and health. Christ too recognizes his body like a temple'."

CHAPTER 19

THE BODY TEMPLE

Our purpose was to make love to the world as we encountered staggering secrets

The collective Indian mind carries a great wealth of truth, inspiration and enlightenment that assisted us into the unknown reaches of our minds, the unexplored depths of our soul. Our purpose was to make love to the world as we encountered staggering secrets yet to be uncovered. Intrigued as to why Indian men and women are much more in touch with themselves and aware of the presentation of self through mindfulness, and their overwhelming spirituality seem to give them greater ability to infer other people's thoughts.

Finding ourselves sitting in the Ayurvedic meditation sanctuary garden, constantly exploring ourselves stimulated by the old city of Amritsar where one finds beauty and inspiration even in its decaying character. Prosperity had introduced us to his friend Shiva, a young vibrant Hindu scholar and PhD candidate researching ancient Vedic preventative medicine. He enamoured me by his splendidly designed golden leaf ear cuff only worn by distinguished Hindu scholars, his many-sided protean nature, being adaptable and versatile in all things,

Finding ourselves sitting in the Ayurvedic meditation Body, Mind and Spirit sanctuary garden, constantly learning new things about Avatars, meeting them and exploring ourselves stimulated by the old city of Amritsar where one finds beauty and inspiration even in its decaying character.

made him a magnet of attractiveness. His stories transported people to another place, they made you sit up and take notice.

Prosperity would be joining us after he finished massaging an important well-paying client who required special attention and treatment. For now, it was the four of us - Ajay, Krishna, Darius and me. We continued the exploration of ourselves with Shiva being the catalyst in the choice of subject matter, but in the end, I thought it was his imagination that created something out of nothing igniting an authentic intelligent humorous thought, I had always found that stimulating some sensory detail had great merit. We'd planned to ritually drink the ancient *Soma* nectar, a powerful priestly drink made from a mixture of secret herbs concocted by Shiva, the effect is not dissimilar to caffeine without the shakes, inducing a languorous state of a high elevated spiritually, edging all at once on purity, sensuality and holiness. It is supposed to liberate thoughts and inhibitions enabling one to be susceptible to new experiences involving all the senses. Krishna says that Pehelwani wrestlers also drink it as a power drink before a wrestling match.

Soma produces immortality of the soul, but not the body. "That is what I think when I've had too much wine," says Darius who had earlier told as about a similar Zoastrian drink. I suppose the Christians have their alcohol at church, which they say is converted into the blood of Christ so it is probably similar to the *Soma* nectar. However, I suspected some ingredients of magic mushrooms (Psilocybin) legally used in Nederland to cure depression. Drinking *Soma* fertilizes everything human. It takes away constraints by removing the cobwebs out of our minds. Soma induces warm conversation just when Prosperity arrives, he is always full of positive vibrations, looking buffed and beautiful. We tease, endowed with gentle assertiveness yet persuasive saying that he gets his health ideas from an Indian Priest Physician called *Suruta* who first wrote about maintaining the Body Temple in 600 BCE and warned that corpulence and laziness is caused by lifestyle diseases and promoted physical gymnasium culture. The Indian ancients followed by the Greeks had an inexhaustible fascination with the magnificence of the human body and spared nothing in attaining its aesthetic forms. They strongly viewed the body as the focal point of human identity and that our soul-spirit, consciousness, personalities and even God resides inside our *Body Temple.*

After referring to the *China Study,* a 20-year longitude study conducted by the *Chinese Academy of Preventative Medicine, which* is considered the Grand Prix of epidemiology science, its conclusion is that in the end, a carnivorous diet causes cancer and that vegetarians in India live much longer than non-vegetarians. However, that is nothing new, Shiva says, because the ancient *Rig Veda* 1500 BCE and the ancient Hebrew Bible 600 BC where Lord *Vishnu* and *Adonai* the Hebrew God both creators of the universe and earth forbade the slaughtering and eating of animals. They condemned its cruelty and warned that eating meat would shorten their lives. The vegans mentioned in the Bible such as Methuselah lived 969 years, Jared 962, Kenan 910 years and many others lived for hundreds of years. The meat-eaters live for a mere 70 years, however, we agreed with Shiva that these ages are mythological ages. As is most of the Bible and much of the Vedic writing, they are written as parables for us to live life to its fullest.

The Bible writers included the perfect diet for mankind on how to take care and maintain the body beautiful, avoid diseases saying *"Every herb, every fruit-bearing tree will be your food".* The Rig Veda says "One who partakes of human flesh, the flesh of a horse or of another animal, and deprives others of milk by slaughtering cows, O king, if such a friend does not desist by other means, then you should not hesitate to cut off his head." How can he practise true compassion who eats the flesh of an animal to fatten his own flesh?

The Hindus moved the supernatural such as demons away from health and disease. It manifested research and diagnosis long ago, something we still do today in a modern scientific way. Is anything new under the sun, is our modern knowledge superior? Questions come to mind. Is there more peace and love in the world? The ancient way of health and fitness was more advanced than what we know today where we have a mess of contradictions based on economic interests, what is healthy and what is not. Building beautiful temples of which there are no equivalents today, such as The Golden Temple, The Lotus Temple or the Kashi Viswanath, and the 2500-year-old Mahabodhi Temples were all made from the best materials of enduring qualities, designed by spiritual minds and the God-like consciousness of artisans and architects using exquisite precious stones all meant to last forever, like the 4000-year-old Karnak Temple complex in Egypt. All of it takes great effort and broad visionary minds, rarely seen on earth today. It is these temples the ancients paralleled with the *Body Temple.*

Indians like the Greeks who came after them were intrigued by the state of the perfect *Body Temple*, a body in which God would be reflected, or more profound, inhabit. Of course, beauty is always in the eye of the beholder because every human being has the potential to be beautiful in their *Body Temple.* I am thinking here of Thomas, a friend of mine in Geelong who has *spina bifida* and Stephen Hawkins with *motor neurone disease.* Both have brilliant minds and a great sense of humour, their Body Temple is as beautiful as anybody else's. The mind and heart are beautiful.

The ancients all over the world believed in what they called Chakras. They said we have three brains, *the Head*, the seat of logic where the unconscious mind directs around 90% of our behaviours. *The Heart* because there are neural pathways running from the heart to the brain than from the brain to the heart. *The gut.* 90% of the body's serotonin, the hormone that manages moods is produced in the gut. We knew from our previous studies that modern science verified the ancient Vedic writings that the heart and gut have an intricate network of neurons and neurotransmitters that communicate with our brain through mental processes affecting our perceptions, feelings and performances in profound hormonal activities.

The perfect Body Temple exterior contained an inner perfection; it was direct evidence of a spiritual mind. Darius, Krishna and Ajay have aesthetically pleasing, strong vegan muscular bodies, but more than that an athletic, beautiful body is a status symbol. "But it is not about being better than someone else, it's about being better than you used to be," says Darius. It reflects you worked hard for it. No money can buy it. You cannot steal it. You cannot borrow it. You cannot hold on to it without constant work. It shows dedication. It shows discipline. It shows self-respect. It shows patience, work ethic and passion. These are some of the reasons why taking care of the Body Temple is attractive to us. There are countless examples from the past on the Body Temple, just to name one that intrigues all of us and that is the case of Daniel, mentioned in the Bible, who was desired for his extremely good looks and high intelligence by the court of the Persian *King Nebuchadnezzar* 605-562 BC. The king's command was "only take those strong, healthy, and good looking young men", make sure they are versed in every branch of learning, are gifted with knowledge and good judgment, and are suited to serve in the royal palace.

The Babylonians served rich food similar to today's mass-produced manufactured non-vegetarian takeaway foods. Daniel knew that alcohol and meat were destructive to good glowing health and longevity and against the Body Temple. He stated that he was not going to defile his Body Temple where his God *Adonai* lived with the royal rations of dead flesh and wine. Then Daniel was asked to be tested and show by the way he looked "let us be given vegetables to eat and water to drink". At the end of ten days, it was observed that they appeared better and stronger than all the young men who had been eating the royal rations. *Daniel 1:8.*

The next ancients were the Egyptians who were mostly vegetarians, based upon stomach analysis of hundreds of mummies by analysing the carbon atoms in them, which was primarily barley-based cereals and millets. Sorghum meat or fish formed a minor part of their diet. The battle-scarred remains of 22 Roman Gladiators found in a mass burial pit near an ancient gladiator cemetery indicates they were mostly vegetarian and consumed plant food.

Indians more than any other race that I had encountered are thinkers and doers, and most of them did not have a self-centred view of the world. The Vedic writings of the Avatars always seem to have the common collective good in mind.

Indians to me are a walking past, present and future, best illustrated when in May 2004, a Roman Catholic Italian woman and political leader, Sonia Ghandi made way for a Sikh, Manmohan Singh to be sworn in as Prime Minister by a Muslim President Abdul Kalam in a country 81% Hindu, captured my imagination. That one simple moment of political change put to rest many of the arguments over Indian identity.

CHAPTER 20

CONVERSATIONS ABOUT INDIAN IDENTITY AND STEREOTYPES

"Now that you have been listening, talking and endlessly observing the people of India, who do you think we are? Is there such a thing as an exclusive or eclectic Indian identity that we all share?" asked Sangee, my Indian friend, the one who wanted me to sponsor her studies to Australia. Indians to me are a walking past, present and future, best illustrated when in May 2004, a Roman Catholic Italian woman and political leader, Sonia Gandhi made way for a Sikh, Manmohan Singh to be sworn in as Prime Minister by a Muslim President Abdul Kalam in a country with 81% Hindu population. That one simple moment of political change put to rest many of the arguments over Indian identity. India was never truer to itself than when celebrating its own diversity. The new Indian identity is an absorbing identity, I thought; smiles all around.

India was established as one country in 1947 by Mahatma Gandhi and Prime Minister Nehru. Indian Nationalism was not based on any racial or religious indices of national identity. Punjabis, Bengalis, and Dravidians look so different. Modern India emerged from ancient eclectic civilizations united by a shared history and now sustained by a pluralistic democracy. The population of India is composed of a polyglot of the major races of the world and everyone got mixed up through mixed marriages. There is no race in India that is completely pure. Hence, it is multiracial.

Everybody joined our conversations and wanted to know more about the Indian Identity being an absorbing one. Everybody agreed about the fact that most people living in India identify themselves with their language, food, music and religion, as evident in its ancient ties celebrated through its religious feasts and festivals such as Eid, *Holi*, *Pongal*, *Navaratri*, *Diwali*, *Ganesh Chaturthi*, *etc*. Moreover, all Indians celebrate Independence Day together, giving birth to a new Indian collective identity.

Prosperity told us that India was actually an eclectic culture because it adopted many things from other cultures, like tea, and Indian drama was transformed by contact with Greek drama saying, "We can't look at medieval mystical Hindu literature without looking at the Muslim Sufi influences on it and interaction upon it." Even Indian cooking has fused with western influences; I had wondered about this for some time. The distinctive features of Indian cooking I tasted were usually hot because of the liberal use of chillies, but chillies were unknown in India until the Portuguese brought them and yet we think of Indian food being hot. We don't think of it as a western product, we think of it as the nature of Indian cooking. It does not make it less Indian. However, we only have an Indian identity in India because as soon we come to the west, we are no longer vegetarians; we go to MacDonald's, Kentucky Fried Chicken and we drink at the Australian pubs and do the same things our Australian peers do, the good and the bad. "So where does that leave our Indian Identity," said Susah, "we don't really have a commitment to it, just to the bits and pieces of Indian identity, those that suit at a time. I mean, we want to fit in."

Most humans identify with something or another, a point of reference. I identify with Australia, I am Australian because

I have an Australian passport and lived there for most of my life. Nonetheless, I also have a Netherlands passport. Often my friend asks me where does my loyalty lie; that all depends on the *situation ethics* taking into account a particular context and evaluating it ethically rather than a judgment based on some moral dogma. Most importantly, I am an individual.

Marcel Proust in his novel 'In Remembrance of things' said, *"The universe is the same for all of us, and different for each of us."* Yet the universe is the same for each one of us, we all have the same news, the same loves, the same fears, the same rights and obligations. And yet, the universe is different for each of us because we are distinct, unique human personalities. Every individual has their own independence and autonomy and we have our own freedom to make decisions. Unless we surrender to group thinking and group conformity, bringing us temporary comfort, in the end, we will suffer because we have been untruthful to our own self.

Shakti says she is a permanent resident in Australia and considers herself Australian, even though she was born in Fiji and has an Indian passport. For Muslims and Christians in India, she is considered Hindu, "While I am in Punjab, they call me Punjabi Hindu. Why in India do they call me Punjabi? Because my mother tongue is Punjabi. I am called a vegetarian, so I don't know exactly who I am," she just laughs it off saying, "I just don't belong to any nationality or race, nor gender or religion is important especially in a secular society, they are just labels and labels are for jars and they are handy for researchers so statistician can Pigeon Hole us and sort us out," she laughs jestingly. Many a truth is spoken in jest.

Our dilemma is that Indians are in general much more spiritually inclined or more religiously defined. Consequently, in Western countries, out of necessity, they navigate their lives without much critical reflection. Ajay says, "In the west, our Indian Identity is of no consequence; it quickly dissolves," and here he mentions all his friends, unmarried Indian young people sleeping next to their boyfriends or girlfriends or boyfriends with boyfriend and girlfriend with girlfriends, but they would never do that in India. They do so only as modern Indian young people wanting to assimilate to a western multicultural and secular society. Religion is not practised as most of it is rationalised away in the far reaches of the conscious and comes to the rescue in times of trouble and guilt. Nonetheless, it remains an intimate cultural tie to which one appears to return at a more mature age, as was Ajay's experience.

However, collectively Indians appear to be traditionalists and many parents are arranging husbands and wives. Ajay is happy for his parents to find him a young virginal maiden, preferable from a respectable Indian vegetarian spiritual family. He reckons it removes a lot of stress when parents help choose a mate; it lessens the chance of devastating rejection. He remembers the days when he was a busy boy at a South Yarra night club, how women and young girls would throw themselves at him for all the wrong reasons, the short-lived pleasures with the consequential broken hearts and pregnancies. Often Indian boys would get Australian girls pregnant to gain permanent residency. Darius recollected an experience with Ajay in an Ice-cream Parlour at the Queenscliff Yacht club. The many-flavoured ice creams were scooped and served and licked by two blonde 17 and 18-year-old women. They were wearing the lowest cut tops, the shortest ragged denim shorts and of special note, they wore the reddest of lipsticks on their tulip-like lips. Darius received a small portion of ice cream and no smile or a look. The two girls were overwhelmed with Ajay's body and personality and showed no modesty, unconsciously licking their lips, almost swooning and giving their mobile number to meet up after work. Ajay too was tempted and said, "Well, you can, but I am going home." He found these kinds of women lusting after him constantly nerve-wracking and longs for the traditions of India, especially at Beas and the community at Dera.

Dhruv related to his experience of identity conflict, on how much he wanted to fit in and look like his peers. He even used skin-whitening cream in order to be more attractive to European white women. He says that he had a confused identity; he applied what he thought was an Indian cultural identity, but now he realizes that his identity is a human, a personal identity, his own unique self because, in the end, all humans want the same things. Skin-whitening cream is used by many Asian people. The creams are widely advertised in Asian newspapers. What does that say about the desired look, as do many Indian-Australians who want to look like any white Australian? Regretfully, little realizing that Australians are *"every colour"* equally and our indigenous dark skin Australians probably migrated from the Indian sub-continent 40 odd thousand years ago. White Australians came here barely 250 years ago so we whites are second-hand Australians, the Aboriginals, first-class Australians.

Darius laughed as he was a Dutch-Australian-Persian. What a mix-up, a hotchpotch of races, cultures and genes he is, "but what a wonderful specimen of humanity he is," said Tey, our Hindu priest who had joined our conversations on what we thought about India.

Shakti, my Indian friend whom I met on the train travelling to Melbourne in Chapter 2 of this book asked what I thought of negative Indian stereotypes. I told her that all of the negative Indian stereotypes are racist, sexist, perpetuated in bias, prejudiced ignorant minds. Usually, these minds take an *Apu* in The Simpsons, or the *Babu Bhatt* character in Seinfeld, not to mention *the Kumars at No.42*. "Do these families and personages represent India," I asked, "or more aptly, do you young Indian people in these stereotypes, do they really represent you, are you an Indian like them?" Stereotypical Hindi *singing* accents such as portrayed on British and American TV, I did not meet one Indian that *sings* their words. People who use stereotypes even for fun show their inbuilt prejudices and emotional inclinations. Intelligent, critical thinkers would not say Indians are "Curry chewers and curry crushers", all Indians are snake charmers. Slumdog Millionaire shows mass poverty and slums, all of these are loaded terms appealing to emotions and not to reason or truth.

Of course, every race and nation have their negative, untruthful stereotypes such as, all blonds are dumb, all redheads are sluts, Christians are homophobes, guys are messy and unclean, girls are good at sports, all teenagers are rebels, men who are pink are effeminate, etc.

Stereotypes don't just affect how people are perceived by others. Negative stereotypes distort how people view themselves. However, even people who do live up to positive stereotypes can't win because when you fulfil a positive stereotype, you might not get credit for the effort you put in. And your success might solidify the stereotypes in peoples' mind, leaving less room for them to think of you as your own person.

So what is an Australian identity? We are many.

And what is the Indian Identity? We are many too.

We are one, but we are many
And from all the lands on earth, we come
We'll share a dream and sing with one voice, "I am, you are, we are Australian".

Song writers: Bruce Woodley/Dobe Newton BMG Rights Managements

CHAPTER 21

MY EYES ARE NO LONGER VIRGIN

An Ancient Indian Greek Symposium, Taxila, world's oldest 4000-year University

My Indian journey has come to an end, but not my Indian story, and not before attending an Ancient Indian *Plato-style symposium* where we met more extraordinary Indian people. Here at the symposium, I learnt that the present is what the past has produced, realizing that these Ancient Indians had superhuman intellects encrypted by almost superhuman wisdom. Here I learnt to pose questions that encouraged others to think deeply beyond superficialities what they care about and articulate their ideas.

I felt like the Dionysus, a Greek God, coming out of India, clad in multi-coloured silks, laden with bracelets and rings, his eyes ringed with black, his fingernails painted crimson. Dionysus, the god of ecstatic and a visionary, the god of wine and revelry of ascending life, of joy and action, of ecstatic motion and inspiration, of instinct and adventure and dauntless suffering, the god of song and music and dance. As Dionysus came out of India, his adornments fell off. He stood naked at Eleusis...turned into Apollo, the god of serene beauty. (A quote from the Odyssey translated by Nikos Kazantzakis, Touchstone Book 1958)

My Indian journey has come to an end, but not my Indian story, and not before attending an Ancient Indian Plato style symposium where we met more extraordinary Indian people. Here at the symposium, I learnt that the presence is what the past has produced, realizing that these Ancients Indians had superhuman intellects encrypted by an almost superhuman wisdom.

After our massages and caring for our *Body Temple* had finished, we moved to the cool gardens of an ancient Hindu temple for a type of *Plato's Symposium* Indian style, where western and Indian ideas are discussed. Many of the new things we heard had been passed on via thousands of years of oral history, traditions first were written down in the Vedic oracles, much the same as the oral histories of people were recorded in The Bible and the oral histories of indigenous people, the world over. The posing of questions encouraged us to think beyond the superficial. This old temple made one feel that one was residing in the body of God and God in our body, sensing that good karma was hanging off every Temple Art symbol depicting the Hindu way of life as I had experienced it. Yet the sacredness of all life was paramount in these symbols of non-violence and the inviolateness of animals. Here we were encouraged to tap into the wisdom of the ages, reflecting and purifying our minds to trigger the processes of inner realization and self-actualization. The right place for a Plato Symposium. Unlike ancient Greece, in the Indian Symposium, women were welcomed.

To create an ancient Symposium setting, Shiva, our Hindu scholar friend introduced his interesting friend, Ganymede, a Greek Philosopher who talked about the comparisons between Greek Mythology and Indian mythology as far as their Gods and avatars. I was a bit stunned that his name was Ganymede who was the lover of Greek God Zeus. Not that it dawned on many of the people present, Zeus had his equivalent with Indra; they had the same weapons and both lived in Holy Mountains; Indra at Mount Meru, Zeus at Mount Olympus. Then there is Hermes and Narda, both are messengers of Gods. Also, they are the sons of a powerful God, shrewd and cunning, tricking people with words. Hephaestus and Vishwakarma were the Gods of machines. He also told us about the Trojan War and Ramayana. These great wars were fought because of women.

The only difference is that Ravana kidnapped Sita and Helen ran away with Paris.

Shiva immediately began by stimulating our thoughts and desires, creating a feeling of wonderment and surprise when he said that the motto of the 4000-year-old Taxila University was *"Half knowledge is dangerous, seek for truth"*. Up until this time I had never heard of this ancient university of *Taxila* founded in 515 BCE when it became the greatest learning centre in the region of northern India, renowned for science, especially medicine, and the arts. Religious and secular subject were taught as well as archery and astrology. There were schools of nutrition, a law school, medical school, and school of fine arts, hunting and elephant lore, mathematics and economics, and schools of the Ancient scriptures. Students had to be smart and intelligent and over 16 years of age. For the poor, scholarships and sponsorships were offered.

It had a yearly enrolment of ten thousand students from all over the known world, attended from as far away as Ancient Greece. Legend says that Lord Buddha also attended but certainly his disciples did as is evident by stone carvings of students attending with books in their hands. The who's who of famous students from Taxila University was read out: *Chacara* the Ayurvedic healer. *Panini* the grammarian who codified rules that would define classical Sanskrit. *King Pasenadi of* Kosala, a close friend of Buddha. *Jivika,* Buddha's physician. *Prince Chandragupta,* the founder of the ancient Indian largest ever Maurya Empire on the Indian sub-continent and then according to Jain sources, he renounced it all and became a monk. Plutarch wrote that Alexander the Great met with students of Taxila.

The University at *Taxila* had a great influence on Hindu culture and the development of the Sanskrit language. They were also big into scientific enquiries and research and we can see that influence – the Theory of Evolution fitted in perfectly with Hindu philosophy. The Hindu evolutionary timeline is much closer to today's scientific timelines suggesting that the Big Bang is not the beginning of everything but just the start of a present-day cycle preceded by an infinite number of universes and to be followed by another infinite number of universes. Isn't that what modern Astrological science tells us today while Christianity is still at odds with science as millions of Christians still believe in 6000-year-young earth and do not believe in the Theory of Evolution?

Taxila university teachings were big on the environment; farming and irrigation technology was taught and practised as evident by the thousand-year-old irrigation channels we saw on Punjabi farms bearing witness of sound environmental scientific farming and land management technology. We could not help thinking back to Australia in the state of Victoria around Swanhill where white settlers destroyed hundreds of square kilometres by over-irrigating their crops, raising the saltwater table level reaching the deep roots of ancient trees killing thousands of trees, leaving the land desolate like salt pans. The Indigenous people had lived and cared for their land for thousands of years, "then, the whites came with their arrogance and ignorance, but they had no reference to *Taxila*. However, even if they did, would they have taken notice of this ancient knowledge?" Darius observed. Guru Nanak, 400 odd years ago was cognisant and influenced by *Taxila*. Consequently, he wrote 974 hymns about the preservation of nature and planting more trees '*pavan guru pani, mata dharat mahat*' he recited. In Punjabi, it means 'air is the guru, water the father, and the earth is the great mother'. India has broken its own world record by planting 66 million trees in just 12 hours. According to India's Government official, this is an act to honour a pledge made at the Paris Climate Change Conference. More than 1.5 million volunteers were involved in this huge operation. Volunteers in India planted more than 66 million trees in just 12 hours in a record-breaking environmental drive. The United Nations is praising India for planting more trees than any Nation on earth, with China following a close second. Satellite pictures from NASA showed a definite greening in India and China while Australia and the Amazon region showed massive deforestation. They need to plant trees, said Darius as the climate change is fast happening, the temperatures in Punjab and Northern India is creeping to an average temperature of 45 degrees Centigrade.

Shiva and Ganymede shared an interesting point that at Taxila, in the Vedic literature records reveal that there was already the beginnings of a participative democracy built upon people's trust. In ancient times, populations could settle anywhere. They lived where no borders and passports or visa were required as we do today. We pondered how is it that a country with 1.3 billion people and the world's biggest functioning democracy in which every stratum of its citizen seems eager to be involved in shaping their environment and nation. I resonated with ordinary Indian people, I perceived that they believed, like I do, that most people are good and true, but it is not what the powerbrokers such as the media and politicians think. It is they who deliberately sow discord by intrigue or downright lies, believing that it is in their interest to create dissonance of fear in order to control ordinary, good people. Hence, there is generally a collective view that if we believe that society is corrupt or distrustful, then we tend to behave accordingly, protecting ourselves against such, submitting to repressive laws usually at the expense of our integrity. On the other hand, people who value human beings as themselves have a more positive outlook and are better adjusted and happier than those who have a negative view of humanity. We saw with our own eyes good communities such as the *Dera Community* at Beas, and there are hundreds of such communities all over the world. Therefore, they say we need managers, politicians,

CEOs, and auditors to control the multitude treating us like idiots. The facts are that most people on earth are trustworthy. I learnt at the symposium that ancient Vedic literature records reveal there was already a participative democracy based upon trust.

Atheists such as Richard Dawkins, Sam Harris and Dan Dennett see religion as primitive cosmology and often politically and socially repressive; that's their opinion, which is not too different than that of those British missionaries who thought that their religion and western culture was far superior to any other culture. It is obvious to us that they had never considered what was taught at *Taxila* University thousands of years ago. Atheists tend to be cut out of the same cloth. Both belief systems failed to realize the fact that there is a very advanced culture.

Through this university, spanning thousands of years of influence, India increased its intellectual capital such as creativity, imagination, leadership, analysing, and telling jokes. India as the leading ancient culture also has thousands of years of acquired scientific and spiritual writing contained in the massive tomes of Vedic writings.

This is the end; my eyes are no longer virgin. India has opened my mind and enlightened me to new vistas of possibilities when I realized that India is the cradle of the human race, the birthplace of human speech, the mother of history, the grandmother of legends, and the great grandmother of tradition written up in the Rig Veda, the oldest book in the human library; it is dated 4000 years ago, but on the basis of astronomical calculations, it dates back 8000 years.

GLOSSARY OF WORDS USED

Adonai – The Hebrew/Christian term for their God.

Animism – a spiritual belief that objects, such as jewellery, possess a divine spiritual essence.

Ashram – a spiritual town, monastery, hermitage in India where spiritual and physical exercises take place and mostly vegan foods are eaten but not always.

Avatar – God transforming in a human form.

Ayurveda or Ayurvedic medicine – is a system of traditional medicine originating in India. There are various treatments, Yoga, massage, acupuncture and a very large range of herbal medicines to encourage health and well-being. The oldest medical system in the world.

Baby Boomer Generation – Born between 1944 and 1964. 55-75 years old.

Bogan – uncultured, ignorant; no manners or respect; usually the lowest common denominator of Australian Society.

Bromance – as non-sexual *bromance relationship* can have nice tints of romance, you might give a flower, some male fragrance, a box of high-quality Belgian chocolates; it is honest conversations about everything; it is a very close friendship between male friends.

China Study – a 20-year longitude study conducted by the *Chinese Academy of Preventative Medicine* and is considered the Grand Prix of epidemiology science and its conclusion is that in the end, a carnivorous diet causes cancer and that vegetarians in India live much longer.

Dera or Dehra – is a Saraiki-language word meaning camp or settlement spiritual town. In Punjabi, it is usually used as a place where people meet, meditate and socialise, such as the Radha Soami Satsang in Beas.

Dimorphism – the existence of two different forms, colour, size, different sexual organs in the same species/population.

Drag Queen – performance artist, almost always male, who dress in women's clothing and often act with exaggerated femininity and in feminine gender roles. Dame Edna Average is an Australian Drag Queen Icon whose real name is Barry Humphries.

Dream time – The Dreamtime is the period in which life was created according to Aboriginal culture. Dreaming is the word used to explain how life came to be; it is the stories and beliefs behind creation. It is called different names in different Aboriginal languages.

Eco–Architecture – Beas Hospital's sustainable architecture that seeks to minimize the negative environmental impact of buildings by efficiency and moderation in the use of materials, energy and be part of the ecosystem at large.

Emotional Intelligence – The capacity to be aware of, control, and express one's emotions, and to handle interpersonal relationships judiciously and empathetically.

Generation X – Born 1965-1980. 38-53 years old.

Hammans – Middle-East communal bath-house used for hygiene, socializing and relaxation.

Heteronormative – is the belief that heterosexuality is the norm or default sexual orientation. It assumes that sexual and marital relations are most fitting between people of the opposite sex. Heteronormative is often linked to heterosexism and homophobia.

Hijras – 4000-year-old Indian transgender community worshipping Avatar Lord Shiva who is half male/female.

IELTS – an exam, International English Language Testing System.

Kamasutra – The Kamasutra is an ancient Indian Sanskrit text on sexuality, eroticism and emotional fulfilment in life.

Left-Leftie – Australian slang for those who are Democratic Socialist, voting for Greens or The Australian Labor Party.

Mindfulness – not judging our feelings as good or bad but focusing on the present. Living in the moment rather than dwelling on the past or anticipating the future. Used in meditation; therapy lowers stress levels. Reduces ruminating thoughts.

Millennials – born 1981-1996. 22-37 years old

Namaste – a greeting spoken and said with a slight bow and hands pressed together, palms touching and fingers pointing upwards, thumbs close to the chest. This gesture is called *Anjali Mudra* or Pranamasana. In Hindi, this means "I bow to the divine in you"

Nath – a nose piercing stud worn in the left nose; it honours Parvathi, the Hindu goddess of marriage.

Noah's Ark – A Biblical mythical story that says the whole world was flooded about 400 years ago and God assembled every know species by pairs into the Ark. Then, Angels sealed the Ark and the flooding of the earth began. Only eight people were saved from drowning.

Pehelwani – an ancient Indian form of wrestling developed during the Mughal Empire by combining native malla-yudda with the Persian influences.

Pineal Gland – situated as a cone shape above the cerebellum in the human brain, also called the third eye. One hormone melatonin is released by the Pineal Gland at night. During the day, serotonin is converted into melatonin and is stored until the next night. Maybe this is called the third eye demystified. The ancient Vedic teacher knew about this but described it in their own language and called it the third eye.

Plato Symposium – The foundation documents of Western culture, the most profound analysis and celebration of love in the history of philosophy. Symposium means "to drink together accompanied by music, dancing, recital and intelligent and often challenging conversations".

Polymorphism – the occurrence of different forms either biologically or genetically, for example, fluid genders; a human being without any specific gender.

Post Millennials – Defining the generation that was born 1997 – present age 0-21 years old.

Radha Soami Satsang – A philosophical and religious organization founded by Param Purush Puran Dhani Shiv Singh Sahib in 1861.

Religion – is a social-cultural system of designated behaviours and practices, morals, worldviews, texts, sanctified places, prophecies, ethics, or organizations that relates humanity to supernatural, transcendental, or spiritual elements.

RMIT – Royal Melbourne Institute of Technology, now RMIT University

Rumination – the process of continuously thinking about the same thought which tends to be sad or dark. A habit of rumination can be dangerous to your mental health, as it can prolong or intensify depression as well as your ability to think and process emotions, it can also cause you to feel isolated.

Satsang – A congregation assembled to hear a spiritual discourse is also referred to as Satsang.

Satsangi – One who associates or wants to reach a higher spiritual place.

Sattvic – Diet based on food in ayurvedic and yogic literature segregating foods that are for energy and those for spiritual development. Food must be pure, essential, natural, vital, true, honest and wise, for example, not manufactured or processed foods.

Self-actualization – the realization or fulfilment of one's talents and potentialities, considered as a drive or need present in everyone.

Serendipity – an unplanned chance meeting, accidentally being in the right place at the right time, like bumping into a good friend or finding a fifty-dollar bill on the ground

Sewa – Voluntary Service to the Master or his disciples. Of the four types of service (monetary, physical, mental, and spiritual, the highest form is spiritual, the meditation practice.

Shabads – ancient hymns, thousands of years old recited by modern gurus to teach affirmations for using meditations to remove obstacles and keep oneself free from blockages and misery.

Spirituality – is a broad concept with room for many perspectives. In general, it includes a sense of connection to something bigger than ourselves, and it typically involves a search for meaning in life. As such, it is a universal human experience—something that touches us all.

Taxila – This ancient university, founded in 515 BCE, became the greatest learning centre in the region of northern India, renowned for science, especially medicine, and the arts.

Religious and secular subjects were taught here as well as archery and astrology.

Third Eye – The pineal gland in the west, called the mind's eye in mystical and esoteric concepts of a speculative invisible eye. Also see Pineal Gland.

Third Sex – where individuals either by themselves or society, are considered neither men nor women. Present and accepted by ancient Vedic writings and accepted by all non-western societies.

Tika – in Hinduism, the tika is a mark usually worn on the forehead, the red dot just above the nose near the third eye. Often given to guests as a welcome and expression of honour.

Wog-Woggie – Australian derogatory slang for a foreigner or immigrant especially one from Sothern Europe, Middle East and India or China.

CPSIA information can be obtained
at www.ICGtesting.com
Printed in the USA
BVHW071015251021
619811BV00007B/299